I0071829

GET DIGITAL

DIGITAL

A MARKETER'S GUIDE

to Unleashing the Power of
Technology

Copyright © 2013 Talib K Morgan
All rights reserved.

ISBN: 0615880258
ISBN 13: 9780615880259

For Ayanna and Soheila

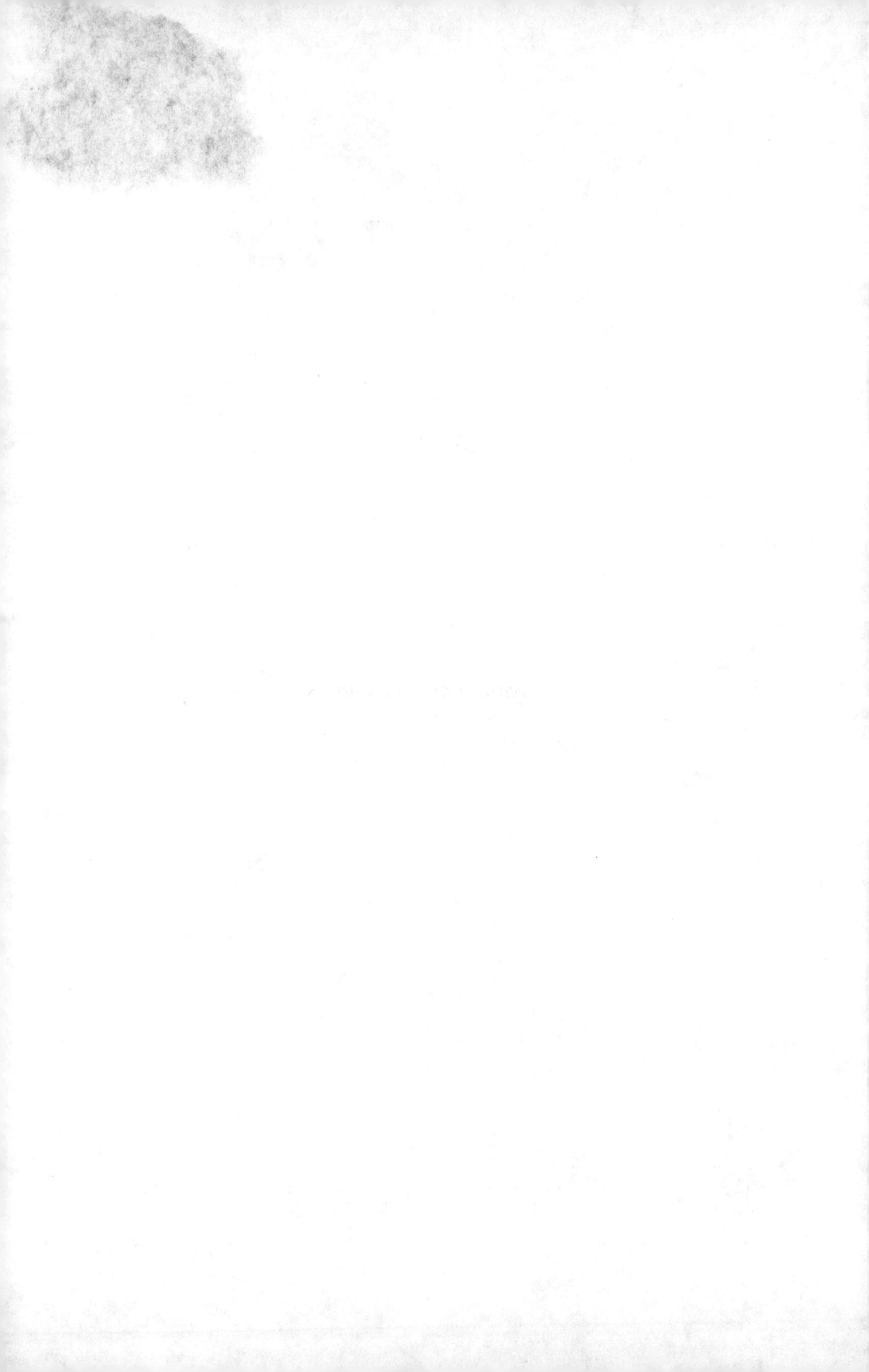

CONTENTS

PART THREE
Marketing and Technology: Perfect Together

PREFACE

When I started writing this book about two and a half years ago, I didn't fully understand that writing a book on technologies being used in an industry moving at breakneck pace is a bit of a fool's errand. As I write, technologies change, the industry advances, and what was new yesterday is an old fad today. It is almost impossible to keep up.

Nevertheless, I finished the book. Working with my clients made me realize that as difficult as it may be to accurately convey the current technologies impacting marketing, harnessing the power of technology remains elusive. It is far easier to say "Let's do something mobile" than it is to comprehend what that means and understand the options available to serve mobile users. An app? A mobile site? A responsive site? A hybrid solution? Which way to go and how to determine which one makes sense strategically? Answering these questions is not nearly as easy as deciding to take action.

As a marketer, you already know that digital technologies are important for success in modern marketing. It is not practical to not have some experience with e-mails, websites, and landing pages. But what then? What other options are out there to help you present a customer experience that encourages prospects and consumers to engage with your brand while giving you the insights you need to make intelligent decisions about your campaigns? Beyond that, how do you build a team that understands both the intricacies of marketing and the details of the technologies that support your campaigns? Finally, what approach do you take when endeavoring to implement new systems to support your marketing efforts? If I did my job correctly, this book answers some of those questions.

I wrote this book to help you, the marketer and/or business person, truly *Get Digital*. My meaning is twofold. Certainly, I want you to feel as if you have a greater understanding of digital technologies and their impact. That being said, my ultimate goal is to enable marketers who are uncomfortable with technology to embrace and own that they can have a deeper and more familiar relationship with digital technologies than they believed possible. Marketers can become digital savvy if they are armed with the information they need to feel comfortable with the options available to them. The key is being willing to take a leap and try.

I have spent over a decade and a half as a marketing technologist working with some of the best brands in the world. What I have found is, as smart as they are, marketers continue to have many questions about digital, and they spend a lot of time learning. What they do well, however, is strategize. They make intelligent decisions based on those strategies, take programs to market, and they relentlessly measure and then tweak their campaigns to achieve greater success. In other words, they operate like good marketers.

I cannot assure you that this book will help you become a better marketer. I can only hope it helps you better synthesize how to use technology as part of your marketing efforts and provides know-how that enables you to *Get Digital*.

Talib Morgan
September 2013

ACKNOWLEDGMENTS

This book would not have been possible without the amazing patience, endurance, and wisdom of my wife, Ayanna, who I'm sure wondered if "the book" would ever really become an actual book. My mother, the most dynamic woman I know, has been an ever-present sounding board and beacon in my effort to finish this book rather than complete it—an impossible task. My boss at my last official "job" told me afterward if he'd known I didn't drink (I dislike the taste of alcohol), he wouldn't have hired me. Marty, since hiring me, has been like a professional big brother. No amount of thanks would be sufficient, but putting it in a book at least leaves a written record. Finally, but certainly not least, I am compelled to thank the partners at the advertising agency, o2kl—Danny, Jim, John, and Tracey—for allowing me to play in their sandbox.

PART I

MODERN MARKETING

CHAPTER 1

MARKETING: WHAT'S OLD IS NEW AGAIN

My first job after graduate school was as a client-facing technologist for the new interactive division of a midsized direct marketing agency. It was 1998, and almost everything about the Internet, as it related to corporations, was new. The interactive division of the agency differed very much from the more established direct marketing division. As you might imagine, people in the direct division were older than the interactive crew, and they dressed differently. But even more disparate were the approaches of the two divisions. Whereas the direct division was buttoned up and focused on true strategic marketing, our online group was keen on tactics. We called it marketing, but interactive marketing was young, and we were uncertain about what we were doing. Truthfully, we didn't know what we didn't know.

Marketing in Days of Yore

What made the Internet so exciting back in those heady days of the late 1990s was that it represented the first new major communication channel to arise since the TV. The Internet brought with it not only the ability to quickly and easily disseminate information to customers; it also brought a bidirectional approach. Brands could engage customers and inexpensively elicit their feedback. The interactive nature of the channel prompted forward-thinking companies to jump into the Internet fray without necessarily considering how to strategically use the Internet for marketing.

Simply jumping into the fray was antithetical to the way marketers had behaved previously. Though some might argue that marketing has always been a largely tactical endeavor, the reality is that a significant amount of strategy has typically gone into executing any marketing program—especially in the enterprise.

Successfully launching a campaign usually meant working through a series of strategic steps to ensure the organization's goals matched the needs and wants of its consumers. The marketer would first identify new opportunities and then evaluate whether they had the potential to be valuable for the organization. Next, the marketer would examine the target market, working to split the audience into segments that would best enable her team to focus the marketing message. The marketing team would then develop a strategy detailing how the marketing message would be spread across the various communication channels through which the target market might receive the message.[i] The actual execution of the marketing campaign would begin only when each of these phases was completed.

Each successive step in that process builds on the phase before it, thereby bringing the marketing team closer to creating a coherent strategy outlining how to best communicate with the consumer so that the organization's products reflect their wants and needs. While no process is perfect, this one offered marketers a roadmap to creating campaigns based on proven marketing fundamentals.

Because it quickly captured marketers' attention, the Internet, for a short while, helped to alter those processes. The novelty of the platform meant marketers had no history of data from which to extrapolate consumer behavior. Moreover, changes were happening so fast on the new channel that marketers had little opportunity to perform the type of detailed research and analysis on which they would have relied if using more traditional media. As a result, many marketers jumped into Internet marketing without tangible goals or a refined plan for achieving their simplest objectives.

The Impact of a Tactical Approach

The reality is that for many organizations, strategy had long left the discipline. The 1990s witnessed marketing's influence as the primary generator of company revenue wane substantially. Among the causes of marketing's declining stature were increased local and global competition, greater market fragmentation, and shorter product life cycles. Because of decreased influence and lackluster returns, marketing organizations were marginalized by chief executives who themselves had come up the finance and accounting ranks rather than through marketing.[ii]

To their credit, many marketers saw the writing on the wall and began focusing on measurement and provable return-on-investment (ROI) for their programs. From their perspective, reclaiming credibility for their team meant demonstrating their programs' effectiveness. Such behavior, unfortunately, represents an inherently tactical approach to achieving one's goals rather than a strategic one. CEOs had different expectations. They were much more in line with Kotler's definition of marketing:[iii]

> MARKETING IS A HUMAN ACTIVITY DIRECTED AT SATISFYING NEEDS AND WANTS THROUGH EXCHANGE PROCESSES

As such, CEOs expected that marketers would aim to satisfy customers' needs and wants through strategic processes based on strengthening the brand, capitalizing on new business opportunities, improving the company's interactions and relationships with customers, enhancing global effectiveness, and mitigating risks like pricing pressures.[iv] Many marketers, unfortunately, remained committed to tactical implementation.

The focus on tactics changed not only the way chief executives saw the role of marketing, but it also changed the way marketers saw themselves within their own ranks. Although developing programs with a certain ROI was a safe approach that kept marketers employed, it did not position the marketing group to best serve its organization. Yet, in a competitive environment where a chief marketing officer's tenure averaged only 18–24 months, marketers coveted the safety provided by this approach.

I would argue much of the safety offered by the focus on tactics was largely due to chief executives coming to believe marketing lived on the periphery of the organization. Yes, marketing created ad campaigns and, in many ways, was responsible for persuading people to use the companies' products and services. However, from the CEO's perspective, marketing was not a partner who improved the way the organization worked. Instead, marketing was akin to a lab where lots of data were generated, but minimal useful information was gleaned. In a sense, marketing was invisible.

Then, all of that changed.

What's Old Is New: The Shift Back to Strategy

The Internet caused a knee-jerk reaction among marketers, who then placed the proverbial cart of tactics before the horse of strategy. Yet, the Internet is precisely what reminded marketers that successful marketing is 80 percent clear goals and objectives and 20 percent implementation. Much is said about how the Internet availed to consumers' capabilities to which they previously had not had access, a topic we'll explore in the next chapter. What is less noted, however, are the ways in which the Internet, much as it did with consumers, empowered marketers.

Corporations, Kotler points out, saw many benefits—listed in table 1 below—as a direct result of greater Internet usage.[v] For savvy marketers, these benefits clearly represented a leap forward in marketers' capabilities. Such was their competitive advantage that even the most change-averse marketers had to adjust their methodologies and adopt the very same techniques that were proving so successful for their peers and competitors.

CORPORATE BENEFITS OF INTERNET
✓ Ability to use the web to create powerful new information and sales channels
✓ Ability to collect fuller, richer information about customers, prospects, markets, and competitors
✓ Ability to speed up internal communications among employees
✓ Ability for more effective two-way interactions with customers and prospects
✓ Ability to deliver marketing materials to customers and prospects who opt in
✓ Ability to improve logistics and operations

Table 1

What were those super-effective techniques to which marketers were turning to find success on the Internet? The same ones marketers had relied on for years—the very same marketing fundamentals marketers were quick to discard when the Internet turned the world on its head.

An in-depth review of the 4Ps, the 3Cs, or defining and espousing the benefits of a well-developed marketing plan is beyond the scope of this book. There are lots of marketing texts that do a sufficient job of that; moreover, these concepts are not critical to success in today's marketing. One fundamental, however, is paramount: *measurement*. I believe it is the foundation for marketers' ability to create technology-enabled campaigns today.

Business jargon is replete with the language of measurement. Texts and instructional guides all mention key performance indicators (KPIs), metrics, and benchmarks. Yet, an extraordinary number of marketing projects are run without marketers' truly understanding which metrics matter for a particular strategy and how to gauge success.

That is unfortunate because it is marketers' ability to interact with customers and measure those interactions in real time that separates technology-enabled marketing from its analog brethren.

---

i.   William Zikmund and Michael D'Amico, *Marketing* (New York: John Wiley & Sons, 1986).

ii. Nirmalya Kumar, *Marketing as Strategy* (Boston: Harvard Business School Publishing, 2004).

iii. Philip Kotler, *Principles of Marketing* (Englewood Cliffs, NJ: Prentice-Hall, Inc., 1980).

iv. Nirmalya Kumar, *Marketing as Strategy* (Boston: Harvard Business School Publishing, 2004).

v.   Philip Kotler, *Marketing Principles*, 11th edition (Upper Saddle River, NJ: Pearson Education, Inc.)

CHAPTER 2

THE CUSTOMER IN CONTROL

Could it be it was all so simple then.
—from the song "The Way We Were"

I know half the money I spend on advertising is wasted,
but I can never find out which half.
—John Wanamaker

Who could blame the marketer if he were a little faint of heart these days? Articles, books, journals, blogs, and every other professional means of information dissemination cautions marketers against the dangers now realized by consumers being in charge of how and when they receive marketing messages. It is almost as if marketers are being pitted against consumers. In fact, the Chicken Little approach to marketing is the absolute wrong way to deal with customers' emerging power. Instead, this new control challenges marketers and gives them opportunities to which the savviest marketers are already responding.

Before discussing consumers' influence by asserting control over their marketing interactions, we should briefly discuss what came before. The pace at which the marketing landscape has changed is truly remarkable.

From a historical perspective, the radio preceded the television as a marketing channel. Initial commercialization of the radio occurred in the early 1920s, though radio technology has existed since the late nineteenth century. Following the radio was the commercialization of the TV in the late 1940s, though manufacturing was delayed due to World War II. Over twenty years separated these two powerful marketing platforms. It would not be until the mid-1990s, almost half a century later, that a platform with as much potential for communicating with customers would appear in the form of the Internet.

The fifty years of relatively little change prior to the Internet rendered the discipline of marketing safe. But the Internet changed all that. Close to twenty years have passed since the initial public offering of Netscape, widely regarded as the moment the world began to pay attention to the Internet. In that time, marketing has been revolutionized. Much of this revolution, naturally, has benefited consumers. However, marketers have benefited substantially—perhaps even more so than consumers.

Despite its great ability to reach mass audiences, traditional marketing (as most marketing options that existed pre-Internet are now referred) presented a challenge many marketers did not realize they had: the channels were immeasurable. You could run a print ad or a broadcast ad, but it was impossible to tie individual exposures to customer action. Marketers learned to rely on metrics, such as frequency, reach, and magazine/newspaper circulation, to gauge potential impressions. Still, such measurements only allowed marketers to estimate how many people would see an ad. They did not know with any certainty how many people had been motivated to act as a result of the ad. Marketers could only hope that they were correctly attributing spikes in brand interactions to the ads that ran.

Internet marketing and its supporting technologies have changed this reality. Marketers now know precisely how many people have visited their site, how many clicks were made on the ads they served, and what people did after they clicked on the ads. As marketing and technology become ever more synergistic (and technology more integrated in consumers' lives), marketers will have access to even more data about their prospects and customers—data that can be used to deliver more topical and personalized messages. It is a win for marketers...except that their prospects and customers will have more control than ever over the type of advertising sent to them.

The Always-Connected Consumer

In the movie *Minority Report*, Tom Cruise's character, John Anderton, seemed to be exposed to well-targeted advertising wherever he went. Inconspicuous devices would scan pedestrians' retinas as they walked on the street and change ads in the Times Square-like world to match the known needs of individual users. As farfetched and futuristic as that idea seemed in 2002 when the movie was produced, we are not that far from such a reality. Privacy concerns will limit our ability to use retina scans to deliver advertising, but consumer connectivity will empower marketers in ways not imagined by the writers of *Minority Report*.

The numbers describing user connectivity can only be described as staggering. More than 80 percent of Americans have computers in their homes. Of that group, almost 92 percent have access to the Internet.[vi] According to the Pew Research Center's Internet & American Life Project, 85 percent of Americans own cell phones with penetration jumping to 96 percent when looking at people aged eighteen to twenty-nine.[vii] Additionally, well over 50 percent of the mobile phones in the marketplace are smartphones[viii]—advanced phones like the iPhone, capable of running complex applications and obtaining content no matter one's location. That does not include the estimated 44 percent of Americans (54% of those 18-34) who own tablets like the iPad[ix].

From computers to smartphones and tablets to other mobile devices, the American consumer is well connected, but the degree of connectivity doesn't stop there. In fact, consumers' growing dependence on Internet content is encouraging brands to extend consumers' access to connectivity to even more outlets. Ford's "in-car connectivity system," Sync, allows drivers to plug in a USB wireless Internet card and access the Internet from both the Sync's display and via a Wi-Fi signal broadcast by the car. Moreover, companies like Apple (Apple TV) and Google (Google TV) as well as upstarts like Roku and Boxee have introduced set-top boxes (STBs) that allow their users to watch, on their TVs, video content from the Internet—in addition to providing direct access to the Internet and custom applications in the case of Google.

For the active consumer, such connectivity is not a luxury but rather a new way of thinking. As is the case in almost all of life, more information leads to more informed decisions. Ubiquitous access to information facilitates this access to virtual information and, in the process, changes what we believe we know about the real world. From emboldening consumers so they make well-informed purchases to empowering parents to make knowledgeable decisions about augmenting the learning and experiences of their children, information ubiquity is equipping consumers with never-ending access to the content they use to live a richer life. Consumers, however, are not the only beneficiaries of this connectivity revolution.

Marketers benefit because consumers' behaviors in the digital realm are measurable. Each link clicked, each topic searched for, each video viewed, and each status update leaves a trail. That trail, in the right hands, can be sliced, diced, and analyzed to provide both individual consumer insights as well as data on aggregate groups of users. Using online data analytics tools, such as Adobe Analytics and Google Analytics, marketers can glean valuable insight that enables them to make real-time changes to in-market campaigns—going from static marketing that takes months, if not quarters, to see results to dynamic marketing where the impact of changes is realized immediately. The power to tailor campaigns to the real-time needs of consumers has never been greater. Never greater, also, is the control consumers have over the data they provide to marketers.

Consumers in Control

Did you know that President Obama recently appointed a privacy czar? In doing so, he has joined Canada which has had a privacy czar since 1977. Like the Canadian privacy commissioner, the privacy czar in America is tasked with overseeing the collection and dissemination of online consumer data by both federal agencies and corporate entities. Such a role has been a long time coming and will undoubtedly be welcomed by a public used to hearing stories about their personal information being looted, stolen, or otherwise used by those for whom they did not intend access.

The times dictate that the US privacy czar is only be the beginning of a push to empower consumers to protect their data. At the time of this writing, the Federal Trade Commission (FTC) has introduced the idea of a "do not track" system that would allow Internet users to opt out of online monitoring.[x] The FTC believes online advertisers have been less than diligent in their efforts to self-regulate the management of consumers' privacy and, specifically, the data those consumers leave behind as they browse the web.

From the perspective of online marketers and the vendors that support them, who could blame them if they have not been as aggressive at providing consumers with options to protect their privacy as the FTC would like? After all, the business models of some prominent Internet-related companies depend on sophisticated algorithms to analyze the data resulting from consumers' online browsing. The analyses are used to determine which ads should be shown to individual users, to recommend e-commerce products to prospective shoppers, and to help publishers present to users the content users want to see. Willingly implementing online privacy management potentially puts those companies in the difficult position of enabling their own demise. From a consumer standpoint, privacy management also has the potential to limit one of the great benefits of being online: the Internet knows what you like.

The features of our favorite online sites are the direct result of their having access to the very data to which the FTC and the privacy czar might seek to limit access. For example, key to Amazon.com's success—as is often cited—is the site's ability to know what we might be interested in based on our previously purchased or researched items. Similarly, the Top News and Most Recent feeds on Facebook are enhanced by a "secret-sauce" algorithm. The status updates of those with whom you engage most are more prominent than status updates from others in whom you may have less interest.[xi] Both cases demonstrate how user data are manipulated and analyzed to the benefit of consumers in both commerce and content instances.

In fact, consumers divided about the benefits of personalization versus concerns about privacy. Results from personalization research conducted by IBM indicate that of the 32,000 shoppers who were interviewed, 61 percent were interested in receiving personalized promotions based on their specific interests.[xii] Similarly, research conducted by Choicestream, a leading personalization software company, found that 85 percent of shoppers find value in product recommendations early in the sales cycle.[xiii] At the same time, a significant number of consumers realize that many recommendations are the result of personal demographic information and other data being shared between publishers. Despite this realization and the expectations concerning personalization, consumers also worry that the data being exchanged are not secure and may be shared too easily between retailers with whom they have or desire no relationship. The fervor of the personalization versus privacy debate is bound to grow.

The reality is that marketers will have access to an ever-increasing amount of consumer data. PC and mobile web browsing represent obvious sources of data about consumers' preference proclivities. Less obvious, however, are the many content consumption channels that are either in the nascent stage of adoption or not yet fully digitally enabled. Illustrative of the former are examples like Internet-enabled, in-vehicle entertainment systems and addressable set-top boxes (STBs), which will allow marketers to send well-targeted ads to not only individual homes but specific STBs within the home (e.g., ads for your kids in the room where the most-watched channels target children, or ads from high-end marketers where you spend all your time watching the History Channel). Examples of the latter include the options presented by technologies such as near field communication (NFC), which will enable smartphones to read data from radio frequency ID (RFID) tagged print ads, direct mail, and billboards. Technology, it seems, will endow marketers with the ability to track consumers' content consumption across both digital and analog realms.

Although consumers' privacy may be compromised as greater access to user information is realized through the digitization of marketing, technology's ability to extend digital capabilities to traditional marketing channels empowers the marketer and presses her to seize upon each channel rather than fall prey to using only online channels because of the ease of measuring performance.

The Case for Integrated Marketing

The implications of privacy restrictions are but one of the many reasons marketers should look beyond the most obvious and most easily measured communication channels for engaging consumers. Yet another reason is the limits consumers themselves place on the content they choose to digest and the trust they have with individual marketers.

E-mail—perhaps the most popular online marketing channel—continues to grow due to its low cost and ease of reaching consumers. The metrics associated with e-mail, however, are a challenge according to Epsilon, a leading marketing services firm specializing in e-mail delivery and management.[xiv] Open rates, the percentage of e-mail recipients who open an e-mail, are increasing. Yet, click-through-rates, the percentage of people who click a link to visit the site associated with the e-mail, continue to decrease. In other words, people are less inclined to follow up on the content in the e-mails they receive, which is undoubtedly related to e-mail fatigue, given marketing-related e-mails are reported to make up more than 60 percent of the e-mails people receive.

E-mail is not the only online ad channel witnessing lower effectiveness. Banner ads—those ads that appear on various sites as you browse the web—are also experiencing weak click-through-rates. In fact, in 2010, banner click-through-rates averaged 0.09 percent down from 0.15 percent in 2008. Any number of factors may account for these dismal numbers, including banner blindness, advertising fatigue, and poor quality creative. It is critical for the marketer to realize that the channels in your marketing plan may not be as useful as you think in achieving your goals. On the contrary, sticking to the tried and true may impede great performance when it comes to these channels.

It is not that these media are not valuable, or even that they are ineffective. The point is that with consumers' interests shifting at warp speed from old media to new media, and as channel fatigue sets in, no medium should be singularly relied upon to reach consumers. Just as traditional marketers relied upon the concepts of reach and frequency to identify the media used to communicate their messages, today's marketers must consider the full spectrum of channels available to reach their specific audiences.

For almost every marketer, this will necessitate an integrated, multi-point marketing strategy that uses technology to strengthen campaigns. This goes beyond simply using hot consumer-focused technologies like Facebook, Twitter, and mobile devices. The comprehensive nature of marketing's technology revolution means that technology can impact every phase of the marketing communications process.

Chapters 4 through 10 will highlight specific ways marketers can employ technologies to accelerate the performance of their marketing efforts. For now, though, you should begin by opening your mind and thinking about what technology means to you as a marketer. Perhaps you are an early adopter, and technology's influence on marketing feels like a natural fit. On the other hand, you may see the gears turning and the shift toward greater use of technology but aren't sure how to make it useful for you.

Either way, how do you use these technologies to deliver marketing campaigns that result in positive ROI? The rest of the book will talk about exactly that.

---

vi.   "Home Internet Access in the U.S.: Still Room for Growth," The Nielsen Company, http://www.marketingcharts.com/interactive/home-internet-access-in-us-still-room-for-growth-8280/.

vii. "Americans and Their Gadgets," The Pew Research Center's Internet & American Life Project, http://www.pewinternet.org/Reports/2010/Gadgets.aspx.

viii. "Nielsen: US Smartphone Penetration to Be over 50% in 2011," GPS Business News, http://www.gpsbusinessnews.com/Nielsen-US-Smartphone-Penetration-to-Be-over-50-in-2011_a2154.html.

ix.   "Tablet Penetration in the U.S. Grows by 47% Since 2012," Cellular-News.com. http://www.cellular-news.com/story/60419.php

x .   "FTC Backs Do-Not-Track System for Web," The Wall Street Journal, December 1, 2010, http://online.wsj.com/article/SB10001424052748704594804575648670826747094.html.

x i . "Cracking the Facebook Code," The Daily Beast, October 18, 2010, http://www.thedailybeast.com/blogs-and-stories/2010-10-18/the-facebook-news-feed-how-it-works-the-10-biggest-secrets/.

xii. "More Interactivity and Personalization Please, Demand Connected Consumers," BizReport.com, January 14, 2010, http://www.bizreport.com/2010/01/more_interactivity_and_personalization_please_demand_connect.html.

xiii. "2009 ChoiceStream Personalization Survey," ChoiceStream.com, http://www.choicestream.com/surveyresults/part1.php.

xiv. Q2 2010 North America Email Trend Results: Steady Open Rates, September 8, 2010, http://www.epsilon.com/News%20&%20Events/Press%20Releases%202010/Q2_2010_North_America_Email_Trend_Results_Steady_Open_Rates%20/p899-13.

PART II

UNLEASHING
TECHNOLOGY'S POWER

CHAPTER 3

WHOSE JOB IS IT ANYWAY?

Technology's Impact on Marketing (and Vice Versa)

Marketers used to have the luxury of not being totally accountable for the results of their marketing efforts. The old adage about knowing which half of your marketing is working, but not knowing which half, has held true for many marketers at numerous organizations. But not anymore. CEOs and CFOs are holding chief marketing officers' (CMOs) figurative feet to the fire for results. Marketing spend has to be directly tied to revenue lest the CMO learn firsthand about the notoriously short tenure of CMOs at most organizations. Key to providing this correlation between expenditure and revenue are data.

Marketers have always had access to some type of data. Nielsen provides marketers with ratings and share information for television shows. Arbitron offers similar ratings for radio day-parts. Each of these could be used to estimate the number of people exposed to a particular advertisement. For direct mail and direct response ads, marketers could easily gauge performance because people raised their hands and directly expressed interest to marketers. There was also the most important piece of data, the uptick in sales in markets where a marketing push had been done.

While it was almost impossible to distinguish between sales increases that resulted from marketing versus some anomaly in the market, the rise in sales (whatever the reason) was always good for the marketer. The nebulous nature of the data made it reasonable to accept that great marketing was the catalyst for sales bumps.

It is not an exaggeration to say that the Internet single-handedly sparked the revolution to change marketing from a nebulous, trust-my-gut discipline to a profession that actually required discipline. The Internet opened up the floodgates of data. In the previous chapter, I mentioned how tools like Adobe Analytics and other analytics applications are used to track users and generate data about site usage. Company-owned website data, however, is but the tip of the data iceberg made possible by the Internet.

Every blogger who sings a brand's praises or complains about a brand is generating data that the smart marketer wants to track. Both internal and external online communities and forums generate data that provide savvy marketers with insight into how consumers view and consume a brand. Social media sites like Facebook and Twitter abound simultaneously with data from user comments and, in the case of Facebook, interactions with brands on their Facebook pages.

SOURCE OF DATA
Company campaigns
Company-owned website
E-mail
Blogs
Search engines
Online ads
Company-managed forums
Third-party forums
Social media sites

Table 2

As a result of this cacophony of data, marketers have had to alter how they approach their profession. In fact, to some degree, marketers have had to become data wranglers. Today's marketer has to wear many hats when it comes to managing data. She must identify disparate sources of data, find tools to help collect that data, and select systems that can analyze the data. Once all of that is done, the marketer has to figure out how to use that data to make decisions that, ultimately, lead to more data. The modern marketer is swimming in data.

Technologically, the source of much of that data is the Internet. In the previous chapter, I touched on how the Internet has radically changed the way marketers look at their profession. What I did not address was why. The reality is, the Internet made some critical concepts more realistic to marketers. Chief among them was enabling true interactivity—the ability to engage in bidirectional conversations with customers and prospects.

Interactivity does not stand alone, however. Building upon the foundation laid by the interactive nature of the Internet are the following capabilities, which endow marketers with the power they need to optimally use the Internet channel:

- **Identification**: Marketers can now learn exactly with whom they are communicating, either through explicit or implicit consumer identification.

- **Measurement**: Marketers now have the tools to measure consumers' reactions to marketing messages in or near real time, thereby enabling marketers to refine and deliver new messages in a timeframe that reinforces the brand message.

- **Sustained two-way dialogue**: Marketers are now able to create a dialogue with consumers that spans advertising impressions and multiple contacts and is based on consumers' responses to the communications received during those exposures to the brand.

The major benefits of interactive marketing are largely due to the way these three characteristics build upon each other. Identification is the first building block. Explicit identification means that consumers identify themselves by providing marketers with unique identifying information, the minimum of which is usually their e-mail address and can include their full demographic contact information. Implicit identification involves using device-generated unique information such as an address (e.g., IP address, cell phone number, etc.) and/or data stored on computers in the form of Internet browser cookies. Because implicit identification is deduced, it is not always as accurate as explicit information. In most cases, however, only one person or one family uses a particular device. As a result, implicit identification is sufficiently valid for marketing. In fact, behavioral targeting, a relatively new but very powerful online marketing technique, is based on implicit identification. It should be pointed out that savvy marketers are able to correlate already existing implicit data with explicit identification data in the event that a consumer explicitly identifies himself.

Regardless of the type of identification, once a consumer is identified, it is possible to monitor his or her interactions with the brand longitudinally, enabling measurement. Measurement is not unique to interactive marketing. Most marketers are familiar with the terms "rating" and "share" that are used to indicate audience size for broadcast television. Ratings, shares, and other metrics have provided marketers with valuable information about their marketing strategy. However, one weakness in those metrics is that the numbers are gathered by sampling. Interactive marketing data are typically gathered for each interaction with the brand.

Almost every action taken by a consumer on an interactive medium leaves a "paper trail." Whenever someone visits a website, sends/receives an e-mail, or dashes off a text message from his or her cell phone, detailed information about that action is recorded. For example, when you visit a website, the site keeps a "log" of your computer's address, the web browser that you used to visit, when you visited, and the pages that you browsed. This type of information has proven to be an exceptional benefit for marketers. These paper trails, in conjunction with powerful data analysis tools, enable marketers to measure consumers' brand interactions with a high degree of precision and accuracy that lead to well-informed decisions about those consumers.

The value of such measurement is clear, but it is the addition of a sustained two-way dialogue that truly empowers marketers and drives the growth of the interactive marketing discipline. Most traditional advertising channels have primarily been one-way media. Even on channels such as direct marketing and direct response, which do facilitate a dialogue, the inability to respond quickly has put it at a disadvantage to interactive marketing.

With interactive marketing, the data collected as a part of measurement is added to customers' expressed preferences to provide them with personalized experiences. Amazon.com is one of the best, and most cited, examples of this personalization. The site uses a combination of consumers' page views on the site, site purchases, and expressed interests via product ratings, among other metrics, to deliver a unique web experience to each site visitor. Amazon.com, like many sites on the web, is built in a way that allows this to happen in real time. For example, if a consumer visits pages related to Beatles memorabilia and then visits pages with Rolling Stones albums, Amazon.com would likely begin to categorize that user as a middle-aged rock 'n' roll fan based on the preferences of previous site users. Future clicks in the same session might feature items also likely to be of interest (e.g., Pink Floyd, U2, etc.).

Through identification, measurement, and two-way dialogue, it is much easier to provide consumers with relevant messages in real time. That's the power of interactive marketing. Marketers are better equipped to know to whom they are talking, have a full account of previous exchanges, are aware of the target's responses to those messages, and know how to quickly deliver follow-up messages that drive people to action. Interactive marketing brings marketers closer to the Holy

Grail—one-to-one conversations with individual consumers, which makes consumers more likely to buy a product.

Each of the core characteristics above (not to mention reasonable costs) is responsible for the rapid rate at which marketers have accepted Internet channels as pivotal in reaching consumers. People within the marketing industry often point to technology's influence on marketing. What often goes unmentioned, however, is the impact of marketing on technology.

Marketing's Impact on Technology

The role of the technologist used to be very clear. He generally did one of two things: he built and maintained infrastructure that enabled an organization to operate, or he developed and maintained software that people within the organization relied on to do their jobs. Whether focused on infrastructure or software development, the way the technologist operated was often the same. For example, a request for some new functionality would come down from "business." Resources would be allocated, after which there would be months or years of planning followed by months or years of implementing the new functionality.

Upon opening their shiny, brand new box of functionality, the business owner would often find that what they requested from technology did not resemble what was delivered. Moreover, the delivered product was often unusable without an advanced degree in rocket science. Such products usually died a quick death, as the intended audience within the organization refused to use it, and the business sponsor was left in the same position she was in before wasting a portion of her meager budget.

As a technologist, myself, I saw it firsthand (and though I hesitate to admit it, I may have been part of the problem at one point). I do not mention this process to poke fun at technologists. Rather, I point to it in an effort to show how far technology teams have come as a result of today's brand of relationship-focused marketing on technology.

Most marketers may not realize that the process I described a few paragraphs earlier has been abandoned by an increasing number of technology organizations. Chief technologists are insisting that their application development teams adopt what the tech industry refers to as "agile" software development methodologies. With names like Extreme Programming (XP) and Scrum, these application development concepts are designed, as the agile moniker implies, to get from business request to usable product a lot faster.

For those who adopt the agile way of developing, there is a manifesto, The Agile Manifesto, that defines agile values:[xv]

> We are uncovering better ways of developing software by doing it and helping others do it. Through this work we have come to value:
>
> **Individuals and interactions over processes and tools**
> **Working software over comprehensive documentation**
> **Customer collaboration over contract negotiation**
> **Responding to change over following a plan**
>
> That is, while there is value in the items on the right, we value the items on the left more.

The Agile Manifesto

As is readily apparent by reading the manifesto, the values of the agile development team more closely align with the needs of business users—especially marketers. This is not a coincidence.

The ripple effects of the changes in marketing transcended beyond the discipline, impacting the technology teams responsible for implementing the systems on which marketers relied. One huge change for marketers that impacted technologists was the realization that all of the data generated by users accessing websites and clicking on ads helped marketers make quicker decisions. The ability to make faster decisions meant that innovative marketers were collecting data, determining next steps based on that data and, often within days, changing online campaigns to reflect the behaviors and preferences of users already exposed to the campaigns. Marketers were moving on a bullet train toward a time-to-market concept of weeks and often days rather than the long standing idea of months as was the case for broadcast, print, and other marketing channels. Just remaining competitive dictated that marketers increase their ability to update their campaigns quickly. Almost always, those changes required assistance from technology teams who themselves had to learn to react quickly to marketers' demands.

Another way marketing changed technology was by instilling ease of use into campaign elements to which customers would be exposed (e.g., websites, e-mails, online applications, etc.). The cavalier user-acceptance attitudes that held sway in the enterprise did not pass muster when dealing with customer-facing programs. Marketers could not afford to deliver projects that *might* be used by customers. Out of necessity, they turned to advertising and interactive agencies whose staffs knew how to work quickly and could build sites and applications that relied on established human factors and user-centered design principles. For these people, user acceptance and user-friendly software was a high priority. That competition with the technology capability of agencies was beneficial for technology teams because it was critical to helping them emphasize usability and strong user interfaces (UI) to applications developed by internal technology teams.

In essence, marketers' (1) making rapid decisions based on data analysis and (2) creating user-friendly sites and applications in response to those decisions have had a significant impact on technology teams' operations. Chief technologists at many organizations are actively pushing their teams to adopt standard operating procedures that enable them to be more nimble and more responsive to the demands of all project sponsors.

For all that technologists are augmenting their ability to address the needs of their business "customers," the reality is, to some degree, that ship sailed long ago for marketers. Marketers have long relied on a slew of vendors from full-service ad agencies to interactive marketing-only agencies to systems integrators to develop and deploy the systems required to run their campaigns. Marketers may continue to rely on some of these vendors, but as marketing technologies and their associated data become more critical to the entire organization, the enterprise technology team will likely want to become more involved in the technology needs of marketers. Marketers will likely push back because they, rightly, want to be masters of their own domain and because they are loathe to return to the days when turning to the technology team resulted in long times to market and expressions such as "That can't be done." So, whose job is marketing technology, anyway?

The Need for Partnership

Marketing technology is, in fact, everyone's job. Delivering effective marketing technology solutions dictates that both the CMO and the CIO take ownership for getting them deployed. While the CIO is responsible for building and maintaining technology infrastructure, the CMO must define her needs and work with the right vendors to choose the right solutions. Some CMOs have long been involved in choosing software vendors. Many others, however, are much more proficient at choosing agencies than selecting technology vendors. That will soon change.

Without question, a new reality exists. It is not enough for senior marketing leaders to be astute strategists. Between the leader and her team, there is now a necessity to have deep technical bench strength simply to maintain acceptable levels of competitiveness with other companies. Innovating requires yet another degree of technological understanding.

Over the past ten years or so, organizations have addressed this need with the ever-prominent "e-business" or "e-commerce" department. Such a department has meant many things to many organizations, but the overall intent was to have an organization within the company that specialized in delivering Internet-focused projects. For some companies, the specialists in e-business were exclusively dedicated to building the organization's online sales channel—often with an adversarial relationship between e-business and IT. In other organizations, e-business team members had a dotted line reporting relationship to both the CMO and the CIO. Today, even the latter structure is being modified.

Marketers would never abdicate responsibility for print or direct mail marketing to a separate department with no direct oversight. Similarly, technologists would never push responsibility for the deployment of financial applications off to a team that did not answer to them. Yet, that is exactly what each group has done for the online channel and the technologies that support it. The momentum, however, is now shifting toward marketing reclaiming the online marketing knowledge center, with technologists taking more of a vested interest in marketing technology deployment. For both teams, then, the answer to the question "Whose job is it, anyway?" is "It's my job."

Marketing executives have begun to task human resources (HR) managers with identifying candidates who are fluent in the languages of marketing technology. Modern marketers must be adept at defining metrics, data analysis, digital strategy development, social media, and the technologies and tools that support these skills—in addition to their specialty. Additionally, achieving success requires understanding the various channels of different technologies and knowing which audience or target population is most likely to gravitate to a specific channel.

Technology executives are similarly beginning to seek skills above and beyond just demonstrating aptitude with technology. Where the aptitudes of many technologists in the past began and ended with their ability to utilize their technical knowledge, today additional skills are required. Namely, technologists are being asked to collaborate directly with business colleagues in greater numbers. Such interactions require that technologists be able to discuss technology without the jargon that often confounds and confuses nontechnical people. Additionally, today's technologist has to be flexible. The technologies on which the enterprise has standardized may not be the best technologies to use for building a web-based campaign. Technologists must be able to advise marketers on how to use alternate technologies to meet the enterprise's goals for infrastructure strength, economy, and security.

As marketers and technologists both change their approaches to their disciplines, there is also a tremendous opportunity to begin to re-write the marketing and technology story. In today's enterprise, where marketers' usage of technology may be second only to the information technology team themselves, the optimal solution to the challenges each group faces—marketers for achieving their goals and technologists for owning the technology conversation—is to partner. This partnership can take one of a few forms as listed in table 3.

Approach	Pros	Cons
Dedicated E-business Team	✓ Strong online domain knowledge ✓ Committed to driving sales through online channel	✗ Little integration with offline marketing initiatives ✗ Risks territorial issues with IT
Chief Marketing Technologist	✓ Very knowledgeable, specifically about marketing technologies ✓ Serves as a liaison between Marketing and IT ✓ Owns emerging technologies and innovation	✗ Limits marketing technology expertise to one person ✗ Can stifle growth of other staff members ✗ Risks IT challenges as CMT executes technology initiatives on marketing's behalf

Hybrid Marketers	✓ Staff knowledgeable about both marketing and technology ✓ Capable of adding value to both offline and online campaigns ✓ Shares technology knowledge among many people	✗ Very challenging to find experienced staff with both sets of skills ✗ Can result in weak cohesion around technology executions ✗ No one has the role of innovation leader

Table 3

The traditional approach to configuring a technology-enabled marketing team involves relying on the previously mentioned e-business team. While it remains a well-proven and popular method of positioning the enterprise to deliver online solutions, it is not without its own inherent challenges. For example, the e-business team is often at odds with the organization's IT team because of the overlap in duties that may exist between the two, given the e-business team's need to deliver technology-based solutions. Additionally, many e-business teams are positioned more like production vendors rather than online-focused partners of the marketing organization. As a result, they face isolation that results in team members being aware of tactical details but not strategic goals. These challenges can limit the success of e-business teams.

Successful e-business teams rely on planning and collaboration to achieve their goals. Forrester Research, for example, advocates the TEAM approach for building e-business teams that have strong relationships with IT:[xvi]

> ➢ Transparency–Encouraging free and open communication between e-business and IT
> ➢ Embedded groups–Relying on multidiscipline, cross-functional groups, and shared tasks to create solutions

> ➤ Alignment–Establishing common goals toward which both teams are striving (e.g., improving customer service, a more effective sales channel, greater online sales, etc.)
> ➤ Management buy-in–Senior-level managers weighing in and evangelizing the work done by the e-business and IT teams so both have the incentive to continue their collaboration

Also key to a successful e-business team is building a relationship with the marketing team. Marketers should be careful not to view their own e-business team as a vendor who only executes programs to match their strategies. Rather, e-business should be considered a partner whose value is largely based on how well they contribute to the ability of the marketing team to deliver effective online solutions. In a perfect world, marketing should ascertain that its ability to create smart online solutions is significantly augmented by its relationship with e-business.

As popular as the e-business group is, it is not the only way to address the need to combine marketing and technology. Consider, for example, the role of a chief marketing technologist (CMT). Initially popularized by Scott Brinker of ion interactive, the CMT's role is clear. In fact, marketing's dependence on technology is so important that it warrants someone on the marketing team ensuring that the rest of the team knows which technology options strategically align with the team's goals.

The CMT lives within the marketing team and reports directly to the CMO.[xvii] The role resembles that of an orchestra conductor for all things technology within the marketing department. He works with the chief marketing officer to ensure technology is optimally used for the strategic goals of the marketing department. Additionally, the CMT serves as an evangelist for new technologies within the marketing department and ensures the team stays abreast of emerging technologies. On top of those responsibilities, the CMT ensures that there is a standardized technology platform on which campaigns are run and that there is a technology roadmap against which the marketing team can plan for future programs. Last, but certainly not least, the CMT manages the relationship between the marketing and IT departments, translating marketing objectives into technology requirements and making sure the two teams are aligned.

Few marketing departments have a chief marketing technologist just yet, but the role offers a strong alternative to an e-business team for the department that wants to maintain online communications under the marketing umbrella. The CMT and her staff maintain the marketing team's technical bench strength so that marketers are free to focus on marketing itself. This approach is especially valuable to marketers for whom integrated marketing is important, as it does not silo one group (i.e., online marketers) from the rest of the marketing team. The CMT has the potential to be an excellent alternative to the e-business team.

As strong an option as the CMT is, I believe the ultimate state is one where marketers are able to hire marketing staff who fully understand the power of technology and its influence on the marketing discipline and know how to harness technology's power to communicate with stakeholders. These hybrid marketers would be hyper aware of the different facets of marketing technologies from social media and analytics to content management and marketing automation. Launching campaigns could potentially be very efficient as the marketers would need minimal assistance from IT or other technology support staff. Instead, they would rely on their own knowledge and deploy the right solution at the right time. This, for now, is a dream.

Every marketer hired these days should have some awareness of marketing technologies. The reality, however, is that technologies are too numerous and change too quickly for every team member to be able to track the different types of technologies that are available to meet their objectives. You would expect every marketer to know everything about marketing technologies more than you would expect every marketer to be able to devise the creative for a print ad or a website. It just is not practical.

Instead, some entity has to be assigned the role of ensuring that the technologies the marketing department uses optimally suit the needs of the department. For many organizations, the e-business team has done that job well and may continue to serve in that capacity. For others, a chief digital officer (CDO) may be precisely what is needed.

The CDO is a senior-level position that serves on the organization's executive committee. The CDO owns the digital strategy for the organization and oversees the execution of that strategy.[xviii] Where independent marketing teams may have to beg, borrow, and steal to execute individual digital tactics they believe will work for them, the CDO is supposed to be empowered with budget, resources, and seniority to integrate digital technologies into the processes of the organization.

Typically, the CDO is a hybrid marketer and technologist with a finely tuned business sense. She is not just responsible for digital marketing but owns the entire digital customer experience of the organization from websites to, potentially, monetization strategies, customer service touchpoints, and so on. Additionally, the CDO is tasked with collecting and analyzing the customer-based data used within the organization. This is a big role.

However the organization chooses to address the need to deal with digital, it is critical that the partnership with IT is seen as a prudent step to building a marketing capability that serves the entire organization's needs. Indeed, the job of ensuring that marketing and technology work together to build a more effective communication capability for the entire organization is a shared responsibility among all players. Doing so optimally requires marketing and technology working together to create a more dynamic and more competitive organization.

---

xv.   The Agile Manifesto, http://www.agilemanifesto.org.

xvi. "B2B eBusiness: Preparing for Online Liftoff," Forrester Research, November 17, 2009.

xvii. "The Case for a Chief Marketing Technologist," AdAge, September 29, 2010, http://adage.com/article/cmo-strategy/marketing-marketers-a-chief-marketing-technologist/146175/.

xviii. Esmeralda Swartz, *Chief Digital Officer (CDO): Technology + Marketing = New Enterprise Leader*, April 22, 2013, http://readwrite.com/2013/04/22/chief-digital-officer-cdo-technology-marketing-new-enterprise-leader.

CHAPTER 4

TECHNOLOGY AS
A MARKETING ENABLER

The Declining Importance of the Website

Think about your website. When was the last time it was redesigned? It probably wasn't all that long ago. Companies accept that they will have to, for whatever reason, "revisit" the design of their website every few years. Over the course of the last few years, I've begun to question this practice.

I have come to the conclusion that the website is really akin to the brick-and-mortar headquarters of your company. If the architect did her job well and the contractor did his job well, then the building will likely stand for many, many years to come. The façade may change a bit, and the interior of the building may be updated in phases to meet new work requirements or technology demands, but the "bones" of the building are there until it can't be used anymore.

The website should experience the same sort of development process. Instead, every few years, large sums of money are budgeted to redesign the entire site. Even if this behavior was reasonable in the past, today it does not represent responsible spending of the company's dollar.

Let's be honest. Who visits your website? I don't mean the sections you've hidden behind secure authentication for your customers/clients. I mean, who are the visitors to "www.yourcompany.com"? Who actually types that URL into the address bar of their browser or lands there from a search engine results page (SERP)? If you work for a large organization, the primary visitors to your home page are likely

- automated search systems (bots);
- search engines;
- people doing research;
- people who wonder what you do;
- job seekers;
- competitors;
- prospects; and
- customers.

Technology has changed the equation. The website home page used to be where you, the marketer, would start interacting with your customers. Today the number of interactive touchpoints and the ways they can be used has grown significantly—forever altering the way in which you start and manage conversations with your target audience.

Successfully managing those interactions means having a firm grasp on the technologies that enable them. This can be a daunting task as keeping up with the myriad technologies that might be of value is challenging for most technologists, not to mention you as a marketer.

Enterprise marketing management (EMM) is a new term for the full suite of applications that marketers can use to create, manage, and assess their marketing programs. Included in the scope of EMM are applications and technologies that include (but are not limited to) the following:

- Web Analytics
- Web Content Management (WCM)
- Marketing Automation
- Digital Asset Management (DAM)
- Marketing Resource Management (MRM)
- Social Media Monitoring and Engagement
- Customer Relationship Management (CRM)
- Predictive Modeling

Customer Experience Management (CXM)

The ability to "sell ice to Eskimos" has long been an indicator of a salesperson's prowess. After all, selling a product to someone with little need for it requires a high degree of skill. The talented salesperson knows that you are not selling the product but, rather, a feeling. From the moment the salesperson engages the prospect, she is creating rapport and laying the groundwork to elicit a positive feeling. She uses the prospect's behavior to decide what needs to be done to close the deal. There is an ongoing process of examining the interaction and ensuring the prospect is having an experience that makes him or her feel good and, ultimately, seals the deal.

Customer experience management (CXM) systems digitally enable the types of activities the salesperson uses to convince someone to purchase. CXM analyzes prospects' and customers' activities across each of your channels to ensure you are delivering a customer experience that elicits an emotion that drives your targets to act.

> # CXM VERSUS CEM
>
> IT IS NATURAL TO WONDER WHY I CHOSE TO USE THE TERM "CXM" RATHER THAN THE MORE OBVIOUS ACRONYM, "CEM," FOR CUSTOMER EXPERIENCE MANAGEMENT. IN FACT, A PSEUDO STANDARD HAS BEEN CREATED BY FORRESTER RESEARCH THAT DIFFERENTIATES BETWEEN THE TWO. CEM APPLIES TO THE METHODOLOGIES THAT ENABLE CUSTOMER EXPERIENCE MANAGEMENT. THE TERM HAS BEEN IN EXISTENCE FOR CLOSE TO A DECADE. CXM APPLIES TO THE TECHNOLOGIES THAT SUPPORT CEM. CEM CAN BE ACHIEVED WITHOUT CXM, BUT IS MOST EFFECTIVE WHEN SUPPORTED BY CXM TECHNOLOGIES.

Forrester Research defines CXM as "a set of solutions which enable the management and delivery of dynamic, targeted, consistent content, offers, products, and service interactions across digitally enabled consumer touchpoints."[xix]

Many of the same technologies that fall within EMM can be categorized as part of CXM. But the focus of EMM is, generally, operational in nature (i.e., improving marketing processes and making marketers' lives easier), while the goal of CXM is to ensure that consumers are receiving optimized multichannel experiences.

In the forthcoming chapters, I will detail some of the technologies included in the EMM and CXM suite of applications. Rather than addressing them in a standard list format, I will use a contextual approach that identifies specific technologies in the context of goals you may want to achieve.

---

xix. Stephen Powers, Matthew Brown, Brian K. Walker, and Joseph Dang, "The Forrester Wave Web Content Management for Online Customer Experience," Q3, 2011, Forrester Research, Inc.

CHAPTER 5

PERFORMANCE MEASUREMENT AND ANALYTICS

Almost every marketing program is created to engage customers and sell more goods and services. No one sets out to create a strategy that results in ignored campaigns and reduced sales; yet, it happens time and time again. At the end of the program, the marketer may realize the failed approach of the strategy he championed, but by then, it is too late. He may keep his job, but the black mark remains.

The truth is, even the best marketer is only as good as the success of his most recent campaign. Where success may be measured by numerous different metrics and various sets of criteria, at its essence, ultimate success for the contemporary marketer comes down to one hugely important question: Am I able to justify my budget by proving the effectiveness of my campaigns and demonstrating the success of the programs undertaken in terms of ROI?

A "no" will likely result in either a significant budget reduction or the end of your tenure in your current role. Luckily, it is easier than ever for marketers to rely on technology to collect information that helps them tie their efforts to actual sales. The key is being aware of the tools you need in your technology toolbox to help you create successful campaigns that deliver your intended results.

Web Analytics

With web analytics tools, marketers can gather data that help them measure the performance of their digital campaigns. The software is designed to measure users' actions as they traverse your digital channels. Each click across your website, the time spent using your mobile app, and the location of a user reading a blasted e-mail can be measured. When properly configured, web analytics software can be a powerful tool for helping marketers' measurement engagement and determining how prospects and customers are reacting to your marketing efforts. It does this by noting each click or action users take and storing those actions in a collection of sequential actions generally referred to as a user's clickstream (or clickpath).

Clickstream data enable marketers to perform a tremendous number of measurements that help identify how users interact with your website and other digital resources. Beyond clickstream, the most popular web analytics applications allow marketers to perform A/B and multivariate testing with content so that you can test multiple versions of copy and images to find the content combination that is most likely to lead users to follow your optimal path and, ultimately, convert. Web analytics software is powerful, versatile, and absolutely necessary for you to make the best use of your digital assets.

Too often, though, marketers do not take advantage of the software's capabilities. My own experience with my clients tells me that many marketers are aware of the need to enable web analytics on their digital properties. They are often unaware, however, of the range of features available through the software. Moreover, even when the software is implemented and actively collecting data, no one is responsible for logging into the application and running reports to gather performance data, placing them at a competitive disadvantage to companies who are actually analyzing and making decisions based on the data they collect.

Optimal use of web analytics requires familiarity with the capabilities of the software. Books like Avinash Kaushik's *Web Analytics 2.0* are a great resource for those who want to explore the ins and outs of analytics software. Here, however, my goal is to help you attain enough knowledge to answer the question, what are the most important metrics for me to track using web analytics tools? What is important will vary from campaign to campaign, but there are some standard measurements you can track that will help you gauge your programs' performance:

- **Traffic Sources**–Users visit your site for different reasons, and they arrive there in disparate ways. *Direct visitors* type your site's URL into their browser's address bar. *Referral visitors* are driven to your site by clicking a link on another site. *Search visitors*, on the other hand, arrive at your site by clicking on a link on a search engine results page (SERP). Thus, it may benefit you to segment your site's analyses based on where users originate.[xx]

  Deeper analysis of traffic sources can reveal additional data that will help you decide how to organize your site and its content. For example, site referrals (sites on which users click links that lead to your site) can be a great source of leads if you tag the user as a prospect and treat him or her accordingly. Similarly, knowing the keywords that result in users' coming to your site can help you gauge the success of your search engine optimization (SEO) efforts. You can concurrently get a rather precise look into the types of information people seek when coming to your site, allowing you to update your site's content to better suit visitors' needs.

- **Conversions and Conversion Rate**–The conversion rate is indisputably one of the best ways to gauge the success of your web presence. A conversion occurs when a user performs an action (or a series of actions) you define on your site. These actions you define are "goals" you want users to reach. The conversion rate can be calculated, then, as follows:[xxi]

$$conversion\ rate = \frac{number\ of\ goal\ achievements}{number\ of\ visits\ to\ your\ site}$$

Because web analytics software tracks all the activity performed by a user across your site, it can also help you monitor goal achievement if you specify the activities you consider a conversion. Key to tracking your success is specifying the correct goals; what constitutes a conversion differs from industry to industry and site to site.

The simplest and likely the most referenced type of conversion is the purchase. Every site, however, does not support e-commerce transactions, so other types of conversions must be considered. For example, the website of a major B2C electronics manufacturer does not support e-commerce, but the marketer managing the site is interested in defining conversions. She can track users who visit a range of products and then choose to identify retailers near them that carry the product(s). A B2B marketer, on the other hand, is interested in generating leads. His goal is to have users interested in a specific product follow the defined lead generation path for that product, notifying the company of their interest by submitting their contact information. Marketers working with content sites may consider a user who signs up for a daily newsletter or "Like"ing the site's Facebook page as having converted.

- **Visits**–A visit (often referred to as a "session") includes users' activities during a time-based instance of navigating your website. Time-based does not imply that a visit has a defined duration.

Rather, if a specific amount of time passes between two page views, the user is considered to have "timed out," and additional clicks will count as part of a new visit. The amount of time that must pass before the user's session times out is unique to each site.

- **Visitors**–The visitors metric is intended to represent the number of visits to your site. Visitors usually fall into one of three categories:

  o First-time visitors–Site visitors who have never been to your site before. There is no guarantee these visitors are visiting your site for the first time. Rather, there is no record in the browser of the user having visited this site before on the computer he or she is using.

  o Repeat visitors–These visitors have been to your site previously. There is no way to know how much content they have seen simply from knowing they are not first-time visitors. However, developers can help you configure your site to store browser information indicating what portions of your site repeat visitors have visited.

  o Unique visitors–This metric is used to estimate the actual number of individuals who visit your site. Your site can have 200,000 visits in a day with the total being the result of 200,000 people visiting the site once or 100 people visiting the site 2,000 times. Knowing which will affect the way you build your site and its content.

Any enterprise analytics software worth using allows the user to segment visits based on certain criteria. Figure 1 demonstrates some of the default segments used by Google Analytics. New Visitors and Returning Visitors are among the top segments available to users. New users and repeat visitors often navigate sites differently. Segmenting users by their visit type allows you to get a better handle on how new users use your site compared to repeat visitors, identifying challenges new users face or content repeat visitors seek but have difficulty finding.

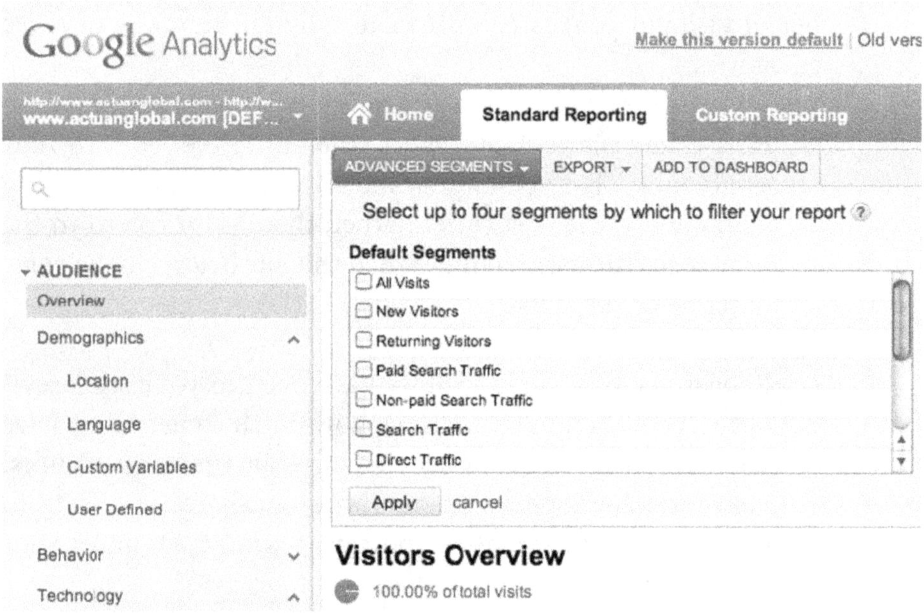

FIGURE 1. GOOGLE ANALYTICS ADVANCED SEGMENTING

- **Bounce Rate**–The bounce rate reflects the percentage of visitors to your website who visit one page on the site and leave. Most visitors, presumably, come to your site in search of information. Visiting one page and choosing not to navigate further indicates users have decided it is not worth their time to look for the information they seek on your site. The reasons generally fall into a few categories:

  o Poor/dated user experience–Your site is not only in competition with those of your industry's strategic competitors. Every site users visit influences their expectations about the next site they visit. As a result, users expect certain conventions: easy-to-find site navigation at the top of the page, a usable search box, copy and/or imagery describing a user-related goal, and so on. Additionally, visitors expect modern color schemes and page layouts, even if they are not totally aware of these expectations. Most users would be unlikely to describe these conventions, but they could certainly identify them when they see them.

o   Poor performance–Visitors to your site are willing to give you a chance, but just as people are reluctant to stand in long lines in the real world, they are not interested in standing in your virtual queue to await your content to load. Modern visitors access your site from a wide range of devices with a varied degree of capability. Building a site with bangs and whistles most easily viewed by users with the most capable devices may alienate the more common visitor. As a rule, I advise my clients to target the capabilities of browser versions released six to twelve months before. This is especially true for sites serving B2B audiences as enterprise technology teams limit browser upgrades and, as a result, are often generations behind current browser technologies. For clients who insist on using "bleeding edge" technologies, I strongly recommend developing versions of the site that "degrade gracefully"—presenting the same content in a different way to users on devices (e.g., feature phones, older mobile/desktop browsers, etc.) that do not natively support the whiz-bang features.

o   Wrong site–Users sometimes arrive at a site they did not intend to visit. There is little you can do about this. It is the equivalent of the real-world telephone wrong number.

It behooves the marketer to determine what is causing a troubling bounce rate. The bounce rate is a barometer of site visitors' first impressions of your site. A low bounce rate reflects a site that hits all the right notes and welcomes people in. A high one, at the very least, bears investigation. One way to begin investigating the website is to test the bounce rate of your site based on certain criteria:[xxii]

o What is the bounce rate for your various traffic sources? Is at least one sending you poor quality referrals?
o What is the bounce rate for your search keywords? Which ones are performing poorly?
o What are the bounce rates of your most trafficked pages? If your most trafficked pages are performing well, identify what's different between those pages and the pages with poor bounce rates.

! SPECIAL NOTE

ONE OF THE MOST CHALLENGING PARTS OF ANALYZING THE BOUNCE RATE IS KNOWING WHETHER YOUR ACTUAL BOUNCE RATE SHOULD BE OF CONCERN. TRUTH BE TOLD, THERE ARE NO SET-IN-STONE NUMBERS FOR WHAT CONSTITUTES GOOD, OK, AND BAD BOUNCE RATES. TO SOME DEGREE, THAT IS SET ON A PER SITE BASIS. I UNDERSTAND THE DESIRE, HOWEVER, TO WANT A REFERENCE. THE NUMBERS BELOW SHOULD BE TAKEN WITH A GRAIN OF SALT AS VARIATION (SOMETIMES SIGNIFICANT) CAN OCCUR.

BOUNCE RATES

EXCELLENT	0–30 PERCENT
OK	30–60 PERCENT
POOR	60+ PERCENT

- **Time on Page/Time on Site**–The amount of time the user spends on a page is often considered a metric of engagement. If a user spends a relatively short amount of time on the page then perhaps the page does not address visitors' expectations. On the other hand, if the time spent on a page is overly long it may potentially reflect that the content on the page and/or the page's user experience (especially in the case of transactional sites) are sub-optimal. Exceptions to this include when the page includes elements designed to encourage long periods of interaction and engagement – like games or videos. You can use your analytics software to identify an average time on page and then use outliers to inform your decisions around what may or may not be working.

  Time on site indicates the amount of time the user spends on your site during a visit. Just as with time on page, higher time on site values are generally considered signs of higher engagement and are thought to be positive reflections of the site. After all, people stop browsing sites that do not engage them. Be careful, though. High time on site numbers can also reflect a visitor thought that the information they seek must be on your site but is difficult to find. Be sure to use your analytics' software path analysis tools to monitor visitors' site behaviors and to identify challenges they may face.

- **Browsers and Platforms**–As a marketer, you would be surprised by the number of web browsers and operating systems from which users can access your site. Visitors to your site are actively using various versions of major browsers like Internet Explorer, Chrome, Firefox, and Safari. For each of these, except for Internet Explorer, there are versions for Windows and Mac users and more obscure operating systems like Linux. This does not even include mobile browsers on major platforms like Apple's iOS (iPhone and iPad), Android, and Blackberry—plus numerous others like HP's (formerly Palm's) WebOS and Nokia's Symbian. Your head is probably exploding just reading all of this—and with good reason. It is challenging to track. Your analytics software does just that, though.

Knowing which browsers and platforms your site visitors use is important because it is a crystal ball into the technology expectations of your site's visitors. I distinctly remember at the browser detail for a site a few years ago (prior to Android gaining lots of market share) and noting how Android device traffic was growing much faster than the iPhone on this particular site. It was an indicator that tailoring the site solely for iPhone users or building an iPhone application without considering Android would be a mistake, though it was in line with what other companies were doing at that point because Android was a distant second to iOS. Monitoring browser and platform data can help position you to achieve a competitive advantage by preparing for trends prior to simply reacting to them.

These metrics are only a starting point. They do not represent the full extent of the data gathering and manipulation you can achieve by effectively taking advantage of your analytics software. For example, the most popular analytics software allows you to segment visitors by criteria ranging from search keywords to pages visited to identify patterns exhibited by visitors with different interests. Additionally, getting the most from your analytics software requires tying the metrics you track to key performance indicators (KPIs) set by your marketing team. As an example, it is possible to track specific site goals—like a user submitting a lead or visiting successive web pages related to a specific product—so that you can correlate web behavior with marketing and sales performance. The possibilities with powerful analytics software are endless.

Getting to those endless possibilities necessitates starting. You and your team have to begin using the analytics system you have or identifying one that meets your needs. Then, staff should be assigned to take ownership of collecting and analyzing your analytics data on a routine basis. The frequency of "routine" varies by how you use your website and your resources, but ideally it would be at least monthly.

The analysis you receive should include the metrics themselves, but your team should also strive to provide you with actionable information. Simply knowing there was an increase in site visitors or that there were fewer leads generated is not information you can act on immediately. Rather, it is more informative to know that more people came to the site in search of information about a rumored new product or that lead drop-off was the result of an interim page that was added before users arrived at the lead submission page. The reality is, web analytics data that is not actionable is ignored, and you should do everything you can to take advantage of the extraordinary data your site visitors are sharing with you.

Vendors

A number of analytics platforms exist for marketers, each with its own distinct benefits. In fact, some of the products below have gone from solely being web analytics tools to offering full digital marketing analytics capabilities. The prices for these platforms range from free for Google Analytics, which targets the small-medium business (SMB) market, to tens of thousands of dollars per year for category leaders like Adobe's Analytics and IBM's Coremetrics Web Analytics. The table below lists the most well respected measurement/analytics options currently available.

Company Product	Web Address	Key Features
Google *Google Analytics*	www.google.com/ analytics	Features available in the free version are sufficient for almost all organizations; easy to use; excellent visitor-level segmenting capabilities enabled by default
IBM *Coremetrics Web Analytics*	www.coremetrics.com	Full analysis of clickpath data; available as both software-as-a-service (SaaS) and enterprise-hosted software; component in a larger suite of well-regarded marketing management and optimization tools; professional services support available
Webtrends *Analytics*	www.webtrends.com	Full analysis of click-path data; available as both SaaS and self-hosted software; strong roles-based user management; highly customizable; full-featured mobile app tracking; strong social media tracking capability; professional services support available

Adobe *Analytics*	www.adobe.com	Enterprise market leader; many knowledgeable practitioners; robust ability to aggregate clickstream data based on individual traffic variables; highly customizable; component in a larger digital marketing suite; full-featured mobile app tracking; strong social media tracking capability; professional services support available

For most enterprise marketers, the options listed above are the most commonly used web analytics tools. One of the limitations of these tools is that they specialize in presenting an aggregation of longitudinal data at the expense of real-time information, which is satisfactory in most situations. There are cases, however, where it benefits the marketer to know what is happening on his site at the current moment—that is, how users are engaging the site. At these times, real-time analytics software is a valuable tool for the marketer's digital toolbox.

Real-time analytics software can aid marketers in a few ways. For example, when launching a time-sensitive social media campaign, you may want to track response to the campaign in real time to assess near-term performance. Alternately, you may be interested in determining the impact promotional content is having on site visitors' behavior, even zeroing in on the behavior of individual users. On the other hand, perhaps you need a way to detect significant spikes in site traffic so that you can respond accordingly. For these cases, the analytics options presented above may have limited utility and are unlikely to be as capable as dedicated real-time analytics software. Here are some options worth considering:

Company *Product*	Web Address	Key Features
Chartbeat *Chartbeat*	www.chartbeat.com	Allows access to more in-depth data than other web analytics applications; strong notification system helps users keep track of site issues and/or unexpected traffic changes
Mixpanel *Mixpanel*	www.mixpanel.com	Supports creating conversion funnels on the fly and analyzing results; exceptional data segmentation
Webtrends *Reinvigorate*	www.reinvigorate.net	Provides desktop client so visitors can be watched in real time; owned by Webtrends
KISSmetrics *KISSmetrics*	www.kissmetrics.com	Works on an individual visitor level; can tie behavior after a user signs up for an account to activity occurring prior to registration
Piwik *Piwik*	www.piwik.org	Open-source and free; installs on your server, and you own your data; data reports available in real time

The options listed in both the web analytics and the real-time analytics categories are strong contenders and considered among the best in their class of applications. You really cannot go wrong by choosing any of them, as they will accomplish most of what you will want to do. Most important is identifying one that suits your needs and making it a core component in your drive to provide your customers with an exceptional user experience while proving ROI in your organization.

It requires more than just web analytics. You also need to find ways to measure the success of each of the channels through which you deploy marketing campaigns. Naturally, technology tools exist to help marketers track user behavior across channels.

---

xx.   http://blog.kissmetrics.com/the-8-most-important-conversion-metrics-you-should-be-tracking/.

xxi. Avinash Kaushik, *Web Analytics 2.0* (Wiley Publishing, Inc., 2010).

xxii. http://www.kaushik.net/avinash/standard-metrics-revisited-3-bounce-rate/.

CHAPTER 6

RESEARCHING
THE CUSTOMER EXPERIENCE

A significant amount of press has been dedicated to advocating the benefits of multichannel marketing. Whether describing the approach a B2B marketer should use to generate better leads or advising B2C marketers on the best way to reach their audience, multichannel marketing is recommended as one of the most important tactics for marketers. It is not coincidental, therefore, that multichannel marketing also ranks among the biggest *challenges* faced by marketers.

Make no bones about it. Effectively executing multichannel marketing campaigns is hard work, largely due to most marketing organizations being unprepared to make the most of it. As you begin deciding on your approach to multichannel marketing, you must come to understand these three key insights:

- *Customers don't think about channels.* You, the marketer, think of search (SEO/SEM), your call center, mobile, retail, your website, webinars, your customers-only site, e-mail, social media, and other technologies as channels. Your customers do not call these touchpoints channels. They use them all with the singular goal of interacting with your company. Fostering the most valuable relationships with them means seeing channels the way they do.

- *Unanalyzed data are useless.* In today's pressure-cooker marketing environment, being able to demonstrate success is of extreme importance. It is of great benefit, seemingly, that multichannel marketing generates reams of data over the course of a campaign's execution. Unfortunately, many marketers are either unaware of the data's existence or otherwise simply fail to take advantage of the data, making that data useless. In reality, the data should be seen as the key to improving your campaigns' performance and demonstrating success to your superiors.

- *A unified view leads to better decisions.* Even when marketers utilize the data available to them, they are often limited to what lies in their purview. One marketer may be responsible for e-mail and search; one manages mobile and social media; yet another is responsible for the website and traditional direct response. Each marketer operates in her own silo, making decisions based solely on collected data. In fact, optimally using that data necessitates devising a way to put it together to get a single, unified view of your users.

How does the marketer seize upon these insights to most effectively manage multichannel campaigns? Technology, of course, is the answer (this is a book about marketing technology, after all). More precisely, the answer is about technologies that enable you to effectively use data generated by your campaigns.

Data is at the center of modern marketing campaigns. So much data are generated by campaigns that the management of that data is at the top of the list of challenges marketers currently face.[xxiii] This challenge needs to be addressed head on because it is this very abundance of data that empowers marketers to know more than ever about prospects.

These data are the marketer's treasure trove. With it, you are able to provide more refined, more timely, more relevant messages—driving stronger engagement and, optimally, revenue.

The most effective multichannel campaigns are empowered by what occurs in the "backroom"—borrowing a term from the financial services industry—of the marketing department. In the financial services industry, the backroom includes the departments where the necessary, but certainly unsexy, functions of the finance business (e.g., accounting, payment processing, etc.) occur.

For the marketer, the backroom is all about analyzing data, which empowers you to make well-informed decisions about your campaigns. The central nervous system of the marketing department, the backroom includes the members of your team responsible for configuring, collecting, and analyzing the data generated by your campaigns. This group simplifies that data and shares it with your team in an actionable way so that you can make quick, intelligent decisions about your marketing programs.

Success in the backroom is dependent upon the quality of the information that originates in other parts of the marketing organization. Providing the most reliable data requires processes to ensure that you are taking advantage of the software applications and platforms that empower you to do the following:

- Understand your customers' cross-channel behaviors
- Manage campaigns across multiple technologies and channels
- Corral the torrents of data your campaigns generate, and harness the data to deliver more refined campaigns

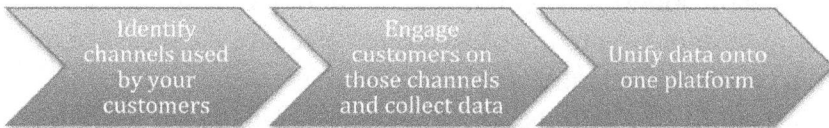

FIGURE 2. STEPS FOR EFFECTIVE DATA MANAGEMENT

Understanding Users' Cross-Channel Behaviors

I had a discussion with a client at a large company recently where I was asked to differentiate between the way people use tablet devices and desktops/laptops. The client understood how tablets differed from mobile phones but did not see why the user experience for tablets should be distinct from those for laptops and desktops. His rationale was that there was not as much need to create distinct interfaces for tablets because they had adequate screen real estate to access desktop interfaces. It is a reasonable deduction. It is counter, however, to user behavior.

One of the biggest challenges of cross-channel marketing is knowing which touchpoints your customers use and how they use them. Intuition may hint that tablets and desktops are similar devices, but a deeper look at user behavior on each platform provides insights that frequently result in customized interfaces for tablets. Properly identifying both the preferred channels of your customers and their behaviors on those channels is key to collecting the data you need to make informed decisions about your campaigns.

Since you cannot easily intuit what channels your customers use and how they use them, you must devise ways to get them to tell you either directly or through behavioral analysis.

For offline touchpoints, you can gauge usage based on the number of interactions you have across various offline channels (e.g., call center, retail outlets, snail mail, etc.). For example, your call center is undoubtedly tracking the number of calls that come in and the reasons for those calls. You likely know the number of outbound posts and are tracking the inbound contacts that result from those mailings. At retail, you can estimate daily foot traffic and count transactions per store to get an idea about interactions. In many cases, you can accurately measure transactions across offline channels.

For online touchpoints, you have the benefit of the web analytics I covered in the previous section. Web analytics software keeps detailed information on the platforms your users use to access your digital properties. Beyond simply identifying desktop or mobile, most web analytics software can specify browser type and type of device (e.g., Mozilla Firefox 10 on Windows 7 PC, Apple Safari on iPad, etc.). Such data are critical for determining which platforms you should be targeting to best reach your site visitors. Additionally, you can use path analysis to get a clearer understanding of user behavior. When used together, these data can help you determine what matters to your users. It is limited, however, because it relies on inference of insights rather than getting straight answers directly from users.

Voice of the Customer (VoC)

Voice of the customer solutions help marketers do exactly that—survey visitors to their sites to get answers directly from them. Assessing which marketing channels matter to your users is the tip of the iceberg for voice of the customer research. It is an important way for marketers to engage customers to inquire about how they feel about your company, your brand, and/or the products and services you sell.[xxiv]

As with any marketing endeavor, VoC programs should not be embarked upon without a tremendous amount of preparation. Success requires aligning the research you execute with the business goals of your organization.[xxv] Forrester Research suggests that VoC is best executed when it uses the voice of the customer life cycle that includes the following steps:

- *Understand your business and stakeholder goals.* Ensure you have a clear understanding of your company's (or your division/department) key strategic focus areas. Additionally, identify KPIs that matter to your organization and your stakeholders.

- *Create frameworks that allow for flexibility over time.* What you want to measure may change, but having a good framework for your survey will serve you both now and in the future. Among modules to include in the framework are overall business health elements that indicate customer satisfaction and loyalty and touchpoint evaluation elements that gauge customers' experience on multiple channels.

- *Ensure your questions are tied to your goals.* Remember that the objective of attaining VoC insights is not just to satisfy curiosity. Rather, it is to help your organization achieve its goals. As a result, the questions you devise should provide actionable insights and help the business improve its interactions with customers.

- *Use the right survey methodology.* Transactional surveys are generally done immediately following a transaction (e.g., a sale, a call-center contact, etc.). Relationship surveys, however, are done in the interim, preferably not too close to the most recent transaction.

- *Optimize the survey.* The survey is your instrument for performing this research, and it must be well tuned for respondents to give you the information you need. In this context, being well tuned means being mindful of the specific aspects of the survey that affect performance. *Survey length* (i.e., the number of questions) is sure to impact survey performance. Similarly, *question wording* can make or break a survey, so it is critically important to test questions with internal and/or external audiences to verify understanding. Also, be mindful of the *timing* at which the survey is administered, as survey results can be skewed by respondents whose situations (e.g., time since last engagement, customer segment, etc.) are different. Last, survey design (i.e., the order of questions, page placement, etc.) and consistency (i.e., each respondent sees the same questions in the same order) are important to survey optimization.

- *Take a holistic view of responses.* As you analyze your surveys' results, be careful not to look at the responses in a vacuum.

Operational activities, the competitive environment, and general market dynamics can influence how people respond to your surveys.

- *Make survey results actionable.* Once the survey responses are tallied, the goal is to prevent recipients from saying "Now what?" and providing them with information they can use to improve the organization's performance. Opt for snapshots of data that highlight key points without delving into tremendous detail. Make sure insights are shared with stakeholders in ways that are relevant to them. In other words, do not give the same presentation to both your marketing team and the product development team; their needs will likely be different. Finally, go ahead and make data-supported recommendations about what specific groups might do and how they might affect change. Such advice can start the discussion about how to act on the data.

Adhering to Forrester's steps is part of the recipe for success (I recommend checking out the entire research paper specified in the endnote). Also important is having the right tools on hand to administer and manage your VoC endeavors.

Vendors

The category of software used to manage the voice of the customer (VoC) process is referred to as enterprise feedback management (EFM). These systems help marketers gather and manage customer and employee feedback across multiple channels. The real value of EFM comes from the software's ability to collect survey data, analytics, and reporting capabilities and integrate with CRM systems.

While EFM capabilities may vary somewhat, the software generally comes in two flavors:

- Website satisfaction: Applications that allow marketers to measure customer satisfaction with a website or collect survey data from a website.

- Complete EFM systems: Systems that help marketers manage the collection and analysis of customer feedback across multiple channels, including surveys, social media, the call center, and unsolicited feedback.

Website Satisfaction Survey Vendors

Company Product	Web Address
iPerceptions *iPerceptions*	www.iperceptions.com
Foresee *Satisfaction Analytics*	www.foreseeresults.com
opinionlab	www.opinionlab.com
Crowd Science *Site Satisfaction*	www.crowdscience.com

Complete EFM Systems

Company Product	Web Address	Key Features
Allegiance *Engage VOCi Platform*	www.allegiance.com	Solidly entrenched in financial services; commitment to helping customers develop actionable solutions

Confirmit *Horizons*	www.confirmit.com	Easy to use for company stakeholders; strong data integration capabilities; extensible functionality
IBM *IBM SPSS*	www.ibm.com/ software/analytics/spss/	Owned by IBM; excellent predictive analytics capabilities
MarketTools *CustomerSat*	www.markettools.com	Regarded as a market leader by Forrester Research; extensive functionality; powerful analytics; deep market research capabilities
Medallia *Enterprise Suite*	www.medallia.com	Strong social feedback and text analytics capabilities; best-in-class usability
Vovici *Vovici 6*	www.vovici.com	SaaS model; well-designed user interface; owned by enterprise intelligence powerhouse, Verint; professional services expertise

Online Usability

In the drive to get campaigns to market, many marketers overlook an important tool at their disposal for increasing the likelihood of achieving high customer satisfaction with the web products they launch. That tool is usability testing.

Web usability testing is similar to face-to-face market research interviews that a marketer might conduct to gauge consumers' reactions to a product. Instead of being done for a physical product, however, usability testing involves a moderator presenting a panel of users, in one-on-one sessions, with a series of screens for a proposed website or application.

The screens shown to users can be from a few different sources but should always represent the intended user experience for the site to be launched. Often, prototypes are used in early rounds of usability testing. Prototypes can take many forms, including paper renderings, but are usually images of user interface concepts users can navigate through with prompting from the moderator. Usability screens can also be presented as functional prototypes—sites that allow users to navigate through the site much as they would a live site but with only certain paths enabled in the prototype. Yet another option, usually limited to instances where the object of the usability testing has been in production, is to allow usability testers to interact with the live site. Each method has its own pros and cons based on your situation, and your usability moderator can help you determine the best approach for you.

Generally, usability testing is done on site at a market research company that has access to users who fit your target audience. The testers are brought in and are instructed to interact with your site by a moderator. You and your team are able to observe the usability session from either behind a two-way mirror or through a live video feed. Once all of the sessions are completed, the moderator will put together a usability report that provides detailed information on how users responded to your site, highlights problems, and indicates changes you might consider. This testing, including the report, can range from $10,000 to $100,000. As an alternative, some marketers are turning to online usability testing providers.

Online usability testing is not necessarily better than traditional usability testing. Rather, it allows your team to maintain its agility while building sites and applications. On-site usability testing requires advance notice so the testing facility can assemble a panel, arrange a date for testing, and invite participants to their facility. Once you have submitted your testing criteria and materials (i.e., target audience, website/prototype, etc.) to the online testing company, they can begin testing almost immediately. Similarly, where traditional usability companies can take days or weeks to analyze data and deliver your usability report, online usability companies can often deliver feedback within a day.

There are times when you will absolutely want to go with traditional, on-site usability testing—for example, when testing your penultimate or final approach, and you need the expert moderation and analytical detail that comes with a professional usability study. Moreover, on occasions where quality is a higher priority than quantity (online panels are often large), onsite usability testing may be appropriate. In other times, online usability should be seen as an easy-to-use, cost-effective way to gauge potential customers' reactions to your company's user interfaces. By doing this before launch, you increase the likelihood of going to market with a product your customers will use and raise the chances of providing your customers with a great experience.

Vendors

Service providers with online usability capabilities are many. There are a few, however, who have experience with brands of various sizes and are well regarded for delivering a quality product in a timely manner. Those vendors are listed below.

Online Usability Vendors

Company	Web Address
fivesecondtest	www.fivesecondtest.com
Loop[11]	www.loop11.com
TryMyUI	www.trymyui.com
Userlytics	www.userlytics.com
UserTesting.com	www.usertesting.com
Userzoom	www.userzoom.com

Tying It Together

Marketing relationships are intricately linked at the hip with the type of experience your customers perceive. Well-managed, positive customer experiences engender strong ties between companies and their customers, resulting in increased sales. Poor experiences usually do the opposite; they drive customers away to companies who put more effort into delivering experiences that indicate value for the customer.

Web analytics software, enterprise feedback management solutions, and online usability sites are among the tools every corporate marketer can rely on to provide a customer experience that distinguishes you from your competitors. The information captured through these systems can empower you with the precise data points you need to make the right decisions about your cross-channel customer experience.

Depending on your perspective, you may question the need for some of what I have recommended in this section. And you are right. You may not need all of it. Each organization is different. It's more likely, however, that you need some facet of just about everything I have presented.

It is impossible to overemphasize the potential importance customer experience management can have on your organization. Companies are using these very tools to perform a range of tasks, from identifying customers at risk of defecting and rebuilding those relationships to finding your most valuable customers and brand advocates and segmenting them into a group. CXM systems change your conversation with customers from a one-way street that revolves around you to a bidirectional one that uses what your customers tell you about their needs to help you deliver better multichannel experiences.

Whether in our personal or our business life, we all want someone to listen to us (heck, I wrote a book to get some attention). While these tools are not likely to be very useful in your personal life, they have the potential to make you a hero in your professional life. You just have to listen—and CXM is a great way to start.

---

xxiii. IBM Global CMO Study, https://www14.software.ibm.com/webapp/iwm/web/sign-up.do?source=csuite-NA&S_PKG=2011CMOStudyUS.

xxiv. Laura Patterson, "Grow the Bottom Line with Voice of the Customer Research," MarketingProfs, April 21, 2011, http://www.marketingprofs.com/articles/2011/4866/grow-the-bottom-line-with-voice-of-the-customer-research.

xxv. Richard Evensen, "How to Design an Effective Voice of the Customer (VoC) Insights Program," Forrester Research, Inc., July 25, 2011.

CHAPTER 7

MANAGING SOCIAL MEDIA

As I have mentioned elsewhere, the rate of change in marketing has increased at an almost exponential pace since the emergence of the Internet. Technologies that marketers must use in their campaigns, lest they be left in the dust of their competitors, are introduced on a seemingly monthly basis. Arguably, no technology is more representative of this than social media. Though a relatively new phenomenon, social media has taken the world by storm, and many companies are capitalizing on the technology to achieve competitive differentiation.

The social media concept needs no introduction. It is impossible to be considered a marketer today without some familiarity with social media platforms like Facebook, Twitter and, more recently, Pinterest. Rather than needing to understand what social media is, my clients tend to be more interested in *how* social media can make a difference in the programs they run.

There is no single right answer to that question. Instead, the key to success with social media varies based on the type of business it is and, as with most things in marketing, your goals. Many B2C companies find that social media is a powerful tool for engagement and customer service. B2B companies, on the other hand, often find social media strategies more challenging because the selling cycle is longer and less direct than it is for B2C organizations. The specific tactics by which you approach social media will vary, but the one absolute truth is this: you cannot ignore social media by sticking your head in the sand. You must begin using it. So, now, we get to the *how*.

Social media is a deceptive medium. Unlike broadcast or print, there is relatively little cost associated with using social media. Even creating a simple website requires a group of specialized staff with skills in design, copywriting, and technology development. Getting engaged with any social media platform typically involves creating an account and assigning someone to own the account. It is this low barrier to entry that has resulted in so many organizations executing social media in a less than optimal way.

I wish I could say success with social media required some reinvention of the wheel as a result of the technology's novelty and the fundamental way in which it changes how companies interact with customers. Unfortunately, no reinvention of the wheel is needed. Success requires using the same wheel with which you are familiar and that I have mentioned elsewhere in this book. Social media success is generally dependent upon adhering to an approach that matches each of the other channels you use.

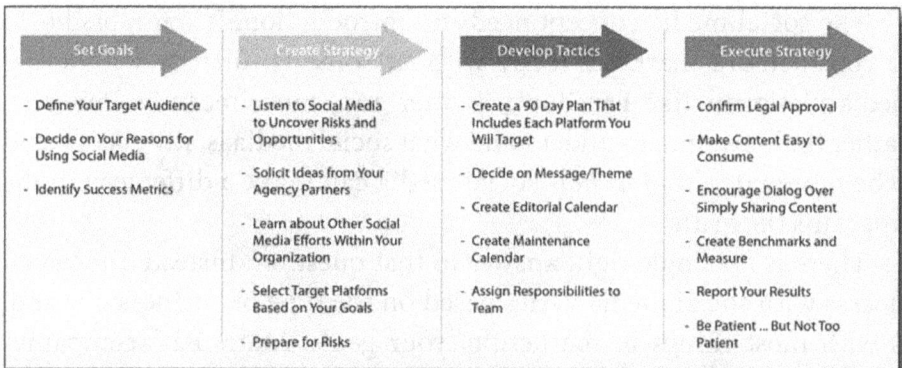

Set Goals	Create Strategy	Develop Tactics	Execute Strategy
- Define Your Target Audience	- Listen to Social Media to Uncover Risks and Opportunities	- Create a 90 Day Plan That Includes Each Platform You Will Target	- Confirm Legal Approval
- Decide on Your Reasons for Using Social Media	- Solicit Ideas from Your Agency Partners	- Decide on Message/Theme	- Make Content Easy to Consume
- Identify Success Metrics	- Learn about Other Social Media Efforts Within Your Organization	- Create Editorial Calendar	- Encourage Dialog Over Simply Sharing Content
	- Select Target Platforms Based on Your Goals	- Create Maintenance Calendar	- Create Benchmarks and Measure
	- Prepare for Risks	- Assign Responsibilities to Team	- Report Your Results
			- Be Patient ... But Not Too Patient

FIGURE 3. SOCIAL MEDIA APPROACH

The phases spelled out in Figure 3 offer a high-level approach to executing a social media campaign. It should go without saying that each of the phases and the items within them are optional. What this approach represents, however, is a best-in-class methodology for executing a social media campaign. You certainly can jump from setting your goals to executing the strategy, but success is more likely if you follow the steps as laid out.

Now to provide some color around each of the tasks in the four phases:

Set Goals

- *Define Your Target Audience.* Identify what group (e.g., customers, high-value customers, customers of specific products, prospects, distributors, etc.) you want to target with your social media efforts. Target multiple groups, but be sure your strategy either allows for content targeting both groups or, preferably, multiple strategies for each group.

- *Decide on Your Reasons for Using Social Media.* Engagement with customers is a much-touted reason for using social media. It's a valid reason for using the channel, but it necessitates a more refined rationale. Most organizations find their rationales fall into one of (or a combination of) the use cases specified in Table 4.

SOCIAL MEDIA USE CASES
Community Engagement
Competitive Analysis
Customer & Marketing Insights
Customer Service
Inbound & Integrated Marketing
Influencer Outreach
Lead Generation
Reputation Management

Table 4

- *Identify Success Metrics.* Quantifying your social media results is necessary today. Unfortunately, there is no single metric that can be used to gauge success; they vary based on your use cases. Some metrics like "audience growth," which measures the number of people who have opted into receiving your social media posts as well as "engagement as a percent of audience," which tallies engagement activity across all channels and then divides the total by audience size, can serve as indicators of your social media success.[xxvi] By using metrics related to your goals instead of social media-specific metrics, you will be better able to quantify ROI for your peers. For example, if your goal is lead generation, link click rates, conversions and sales will likely be better metrics than engagement.

Create Strategy

- *Listen to Social Media to Uncover Risks and Opportunities.* Does a falling tree make a sound if you are not there to hear it? A resounding *yes*! Your customers and your competitors are already talking about your industry and, probably, your company. By using a listening platform before jumping in with engaging your audience, you can survey the landscape and assess what makes sense for your company. Your competitors' online successes and travails as well as the public's comments can serve as a guidepost on how to tailor your messages to achieve your goals.

- *Solicit Ideas from Your Agency Partners.* Just as your ad agency has great (hopefully) ideas when it comes to your other marketing campaigns, they likely have experience and creative ideas that can make your social media efforts flourish rather than wither.

- *Learn About Other Social Media Efforts within Your Organization.* At an enterprise-size organization, there are likely existing in-market social media programs either at the corporate level or within other departments. As long as your company has not set guidelines indicating that all social media campaigns should be run through a central corporate office, you should not let the existing programs prevent you from embarking on your own social media journey. That being said, you do want to keep in mind that consumers do not always see the distinctions between "Acme, Inc." and "Acme Medical Devices Group." There should be some amount of coordination in an effort to minimize overlapping and conflicting messages between groups.

- *Select Target Platforms Based on Your Goals.* As ideal as it would be for every social media platform to be equally valuable for every task, it simply is not the case. Pinterest, for example, is regarded as a phenomenal platform for driving e-commerce sales. Its lack of real-time interactivity and its popularity with a specific demographic group make it a less than ideal platform for customer service, for example. Companies like American Express and Comcast are using Twitter as an excellent customer service platform, but Twitter would not be the best place for a company looking to make a branding splash or launch a custom application. Facebook's platform and its Open Graph data are well suited for such campaigns, however.

- *Prepare for Risks.* The simplicity with which you can use social media matches the simplicity with which you can run into unexpected risks. Here are some of the largest risks associated with social media:[xxvii]

  o Damage to your organization/brand's reputation
  o Releasing confidential information
  o Legal, regulatory, and compliance issues
  o Theft or hijacking of your social media account

You accept some level of risk when you utilize a technology that deals directly with the public. There are some steps you can take to minimize your chances of the risks I highlighted above. First, identify potential risks that can arise with the social media platform(s) you use. Second, assess the risks and assign values to the specific risks to uncover so you can quantitatively compare them to each other. Third, do what it takes to ensure you have properly managed and mitigated the risks you have identified so you can react appropriately if the risk is realized. Finally, review and evaluate your risks and your mitigation techniques periodically as the risks may change and new ones may factor into your decision making.

Develop Tactics

- *Create a 90-Day Plan That Includes Each Platform You Will Target.* The first few months of your social media execution lay the groundwork for what is to come. During this initial period, your staff will hone their social media skills and refine the message to better appeal to your customers. It is also the period during which the most mistakes will be made because of a lack of familiarity and when your results will have the least impact on your goals. The 90-day plan helps by ensuring you have outlined goals and expectations for that period. For example, if you are using Twitter, Facebook, and Pinterest, you may decide that the first 90 days is best spent by phasing in activity across the different platforms, perhaps starting with Twitter and then, after a few weeks, activating the second account and then the third account. Or, you could use the period to build your audience[xxviii] rather than looking to achieve your business goals.

- *Identify Software That Can Help You Manage Your Social Media Interactions.* Each major social media platform has both web and mobile-based interfaces you can use to post and view content. Moreover, third-party apps offer more robust functionality for individuals than found in the platform-provided user experiences. For most enterprises, however, none of these options is adequate for managing your interactions with your audience. You need dedicated software for managing social media. According to the Altimeter Group, the software you use depends on how you intend to use social media. They have identified the following use cases:[xxix]

o Intense Engagement–Used by companies that must respond to a high volume of customer requests either for customer support or because of customer interest. Comcast and American Express fall into this category.

o Social Broadcasting–Publishers who are driving people to their sites to view content commonly fall into this category. Examples include news organizations like The Wall Street Journal and Paramount Pictures that use social media to direct people to their content.

o Platform Campaign Marketing–Companies who develop custom applications and services that work through social media sites like Facebook and Twitter are included in this category. Examples include American Express and Coca-Cola.

o Distributed Brand Presence–Companies in this use case include those with numerous customer engagement centers (i.e., supermarkets, restaurants, hotels, big box stores, etc.) who are likely to have at least one account for each location with the total number of accounts within the company climbing into the hundreds or thousands. Examples include

Whole Foods Market, St. Regis Hotels and Resorts, and fast-food chain Sonic Drive-In.

o   Tailored Customizations–Companies whose needs are very complex and perhaps require customization applications or extensive support will fall into this category. Examples include companies like Ford who offers a robust social platform, Ford Social, through Facebook as well as companies in heavily regulated industries such as banking.

The free Altimeter report, "A Strategy for Managing Social Proliferation," is a worthwhile read for marketers investigating social media management solutions as they provide a more comprehensive list of available software. They also rate each software by its suitability for each of the use cases mentioned above.

- *Decide on Your Message and Create an Editorial Calendar.* What your team will be talking about (with a few exceptions) should not be left to chance. You should determine well in advance of your first posts what your tone and style will be. Moreover, you should have an idea about the type of topics you want to address. In the case of broadcasting content with social media (rather than providing customer support), the content should be planned out in advance on an editorial calendar. By doing so, you are better able to ensure that your team is driving home the messaging you laid out and that the themes you set out to address are covered. Additionally, the editorial calendar serves as a good way to ensure your posts are timed to align with other activities within the organization.

Once your team has developed a stronger social media competency and is more familiar with the type of posts that work for your brand, you can allow the team not to hew to the editorial calendar as tightly, or at least allow some discretion to post content that is not on the calendar for the day.

- *Create Maintenance Schedule.* Ensure your team knows when important tasks related to your social media accounts need to be accomplished. For example, tasks to build your audience/follows as well as updating the editorial calendar[xxx] should be added to the maintenance calendar so they are not neglected as the team becomes busier.

- *Assign Responsibilities.* This is self-explanatory. It is easy to overlook, however. Someone on your team needs to be responsible for each task associated with executing your campaign. Someone will need to create and maintain the editorial and maintenance schedules. Someone will need to post content and respond to interest from your audience. Additionally, a member of your team will need to be tasked with benchmarking and measuring the results of your campaign. By assigning these roles in advance, you minimize the risk of the tasks falling through the cracks.

Execute Strategy

- *Confirm Legal Approval.* Every corporate legal team works differently. Many want to approve everything that the customer will see. Others are more reactive and trust the marketer to work in the best interest of the organization—only stepping in when an issue arises. Regardless of how legal works within your enterprise, you should discuss your plans with someone on their team and get their approval. It benefits you, them, and your company.

- *Make Content Easy to Consume.* It is natural to want to leverage existing content, if you are able, when creating campaigns around products/brands you have marketed previously. Depending on the content, however, reuse may not be the best solution for your audience. It is obvious but bears saying: we no longer live in a PC-only world. Your social audience can view your content on their phones, tablets, eReaders, TVs, refrigerators, and even their watches. Consumers may be at home, at work, in the car, at the store, on the train, or walking down the street, and each scenario elicits a different media consumption habit—slower at home with multiple devices, perhaps, while much more rapidly at work or in the car. Your content should adhere to what I will call the three Cs of social content: be convenient enough to access (do not put hurdles in front of content[xxxi]) on any device, compelling enough to entice readers to proceed further, and concise enough to give them what they need when they need it.

3Cs OF SOCIAL MEDIA CONTENT

CONVENIENT—EASY TO ACCESS
COMPELLING—RELEVANT AND VALUABLE TO THE CONSUMER
CONCISE—CAN BE READ QUICKLY WITH LINKS TO MORE DETAIL

- *Encourage Dialogue Instead of Simply Sharing Content.* When first embarking on the social media journey, brands often post links to content and wait for the hordes to click on the link. That may happen, but it is more likely that your numbers will not be what you expected. Rather than posting content and hoping people will click and share, your team should engage users by prompting them to interact with your brand. Posting a link to some content? Ask a question that gets your audience thinking about the topic, and make the link part of the post. For example, if a hotel was having a weekend special for couples, rather than just posting a link to the page with detail on the special, the hotel could ask, "On a scale of 1–10 (awesome), how was your week? Maybe you can redeem it with our couples retreat weekend." When done well, the result should be a dialogue with your customers and higher engagement.

- *Create Benchmarks and Measure.* Determining the efficacy of your social media campaign can be relatively straightforward if you set your benchmarks early on in the process. Identify the number of audience members you have on each social media platform a week (or a month) into your campaign and establish that as your benchmark. Similarly, begin to track your interactions with your audience and create a benchmark for and then track those engagements. Beyond social media metrics, you should also create benchmarks for business-related metrics. For example, if your goal is to offer customer service online, then before launching your campaign set a benchmark for the number of customer service calls you receive across all touchpoints on a daily/weekly/monthly basis. By comparing pre-campaign and post-campaign call volume, you will be better able to determine the impact of your efforts and measure ROI.

- *Report Your Results.* There is a reason so many television evangelists live in big houses and drive fancy cars. They are excellent at telling their own story, which leads more people to contribute to them. By reporting your successes with social media, you evangelize the channel and make it more likely your management will provide you with an additional budget. It may not result in your having a house in the Hamptons, but touting those successes can do wonders for your team and your career.

- *Be Patient...But Not Too Patient.* Every industry is different. Even the speed at which customers move through the sales cycle within an industry can differ from company to company. Consequently, it is impossible to say you should see great results in four weeks. If you are running a yearlong lead-generation program, ramping up over the course of a month is not so bad. If you are executing a three-month-long awareness campaign, on the other hand, you do not have a month to wait for results.

Now that you have a clearer picture of what it takes to assemble a successful social media campaign, we can discuss some of the technologies that can help make it easier to take advantage of the social media channel. For most brands, the size of your audience has the potential to make managing your social media accounts daunting. Listen to what the marketplace is saying about your brand and engage with prospects/customers interested in your products. While doing that, you will want to track what you heard and maintain accurate measurement and analysis of your audience size, engagements, and other metrics. Software can help you do that.

For good reason, all social media software is not created equally or with the same task in mind. As marketers may have a range of objectives for social media, the applications available to help you achieve those goals vary. Among the types of social media software most sought by marketers are the following:

- Listening Platforms: Software that allows marketers to monitor social media broadcasts and identify mentions of their brand. (Naturally, you can also listen into what is said about your competitors' brands and companies.) The most effective listening platform software goes beyond simply telling you what social media users said and gives you insights about those users and their posts. These insights can be used to gauge anything from intent to purchase to the age ranges of the people posting about a specific event.

- Social CRM (SCRM): Software that enables the organization to engage and manage relationships with customers. Where traditional customer relationship management (CRM) emphasizes data and efficiency, social CRM places the customer at the center of the organizational processes. Social CRM tools can be used across multiple facets of the customer relationship, including marketing, sales, public relationships, customer experience, advocacy, and serving customers.[xxxii]

In fact, many companies develop social CRM strategies to engage customers in a number of ways that include co-developing new products and providing price comparisons—concepts devised based on customer needs rather than organizational needs.[xxxiii] Applications in this category certainly gather data from social media platforms like Facebook and Twitter, but they also excel at providing functionality such as message boards, blogs, rating systems, and social community-oriented concepts.[xxxiv]

- Social Media Management Systems (SMMS): Platforms that provide marketers with specific functionality for engaging customers. SCRM is a subset of SMMS, but not all SMMS applications are considered to be SCRM tools. Altimeter points out that organizations generally have five use cases that result in using a SMMS:

  o Intense Engagement: Used by companies that must respond to a high volume of customer requests either for customer support or because of customer interest. Comcast and American Express fall into this category.

  o Social Broadcasting: Publishers who are driving people to their sites to view content commonly fall into this category. Examples include news organizations like The Wall Street

Journal and Paramount Pictures that use social media to direct people to their content.

o Platform Campaign Marketing: Companies who develop custom applications and services that work through social media sites like Facebook and Twitter are included in this category. Examples include American Express and Coca-Cola.

o Distributed Brand Presence: Companies in this use case include those with numerous customer engagement centers (i.e., supermarkets, restaurants, hotels, big box stores, etc.) who are likely to have at least one account for each location with the total number of accounts within the company climbing into the hundreds or thousands. Examples include Whole Foods Market, St. Regis Hotels and Resorts, and the fast-food chain Sonic Drive-In.

o Tailored Customizations: Organizations whose need extends beyond the scope of the use cases listed above turn to partners who can help them create unique social media solutions. These solutions require significant customization or extensive customer support. Examples include Proctor & Gamble, Frito Lay, and UPS.

Depending on your needs, you may find that your business requires one type of these solutions or a combination of them. Truth be told, while I choose to segment the software into three different categories, in practice you will find significant overlap between those categories. By methodically going through the social media approach laid out above in figure 3, you can determine the type of solution that makes the most sense for you.

Social Media Listening Platforms

Company *Product*	Web Address	Key Features
Visible Technologies *Visible Edge*	www.visibletech-nologies.com	Ranked by Forrester Research as industry leader; impressive senti-ment and data quality
Salesforce/ Radian6 *Radian6*	www.radian6.com	Owned by powerhouse Salesforce.com; considered best in class; powerful engagement tools
NetworkedInsights *SocialSense*	www.networked-insights.com	Valuable media data sources; deep data analysis capabilities; strong profes-sional services team
Lithium *Social Customer Suite*	www.lithium.com	Wide range of capabilities across multiple industries; highly regarded real-time dashboard

Social CRM (SCRM)

Company *Product*	Web Address	Key Features
Jive *Social Business Platform*	www.jivesoftware.com	Powerful analytics ca-pabilities; user friendly admin features; strong support for customer communities.

Lithium *Community* *Everywhere*	www.lithium.com	Strong admin user interface; advanced crowd-sourced user-generated content features; good professional services team.
Acquia *Commons*	www.acquia.com	Large developer ecosystem; software is open source and free; easy to use; built using well regarded content management system, Drupal.

Social Media Management Systems (SMMS)

Company *Product*	Web Address
Spredfast *Social Business Platform*	www.jivesoftware.com
Oracle Vitrue *Social Relationship Management Platform*	www.vitrue.com
Shoutlet *Social Enterprise*	www.shoutlet.com
Sprinklr *Social Media Management Platform*	www.spinklr.com

Using social media and effectively taking advantage of the platform to engage your audience are two very different concepts. Anyone who uses Facebook or Twitter or Pinterest uses social media. As a marketer, you are tasked with using social media platforms to create, manage, maintain, and extract value from social media. In this section, I have tried to arm you with the information you need to do just that. By following the steps laid out here, you can begin developing a social media approach that delivers for you and your team.

xxvi.   "Beyond the Buzz: 41 Social Media Metrics Defined," Simply Measured, http://simplymeasured.com/blog/2012/05/31/beyond-the-buzz-41-social-media-metrics-defined/.

xxvii.   Alan Webb, Charlene Li, and Jaimy Szymanski, "Guarding the Social Gates: The Imperative for Social Media Risk Management," Altimeter, August 9, 2012.

xxviii.   Rachel Strella, "How to Create a Social Media Strategy," Social Media Today, August 5, 2012, http://socialmediatoday.com/node/679466.

xxix.   Jeremiah Owyang, Andrew Jones, and Christine Tran, "A Strategy for Managing Social Media Proliferation," Altimeter Group, January 5, 2012.

xxx.   See note xxviii above.

xxxi.   Heidi Cohen, "Social Media Engagement: 7 Marketing Tactics You Need Now," Conduit, June 12, 2012, http://blog.conduit.com/2012/06/12/social-media-engagement-7-marketing-tactics-you-need-now/.

xxxii.   Jacob Morgan, "What is Social CRM?", Social Media Examiner, November 3, 2010, http://www.socialmediaexaminer.com/what-is-social-crm/.

xxxiii.   Adam Samer, Ed Thompson, and Jim Davies, "Magic Quadrant for Social CRM," Gartner, July 25, 2011.

xxxiv.   Ibid.

CHAPTER 8

MOBILE FOR MARKETING

Ah, mobile. Perhaps no consumer-oriented technology has more excitement surrounding it than mobile. There is good reason for that excitement. Apple unquestionably changed the perception of the mobile device with the introduction of the iPhone. It was not the first smartphone, but it was the one that made the concept of the smartphone accessible to everyone and brought the mobile device closer to its potential as a functional tool rather than simply as a cordless telephone.

It was 2007 when the first iPhone debuted and radically altered the cell phone marketplace. Today, the smartphone is everywhere, providing access to information and content users want wherever and whenever they need it. In fact, in the United States, smartphones are used by 51 percent of the cellphone-owning population.[xxxv] Additionally, a significant number of those smartphone owners are taking advantage of the mobile content options provided to them by those phones. For example, 75.5 percent of them have sent text messages to another phone; 54.0 percent have downloaded apps to their phone; and 52.6 percent have used the browser on their smartphone. [xxxvi] Each of these content engagement methods offers an opportunity for the marketer.

Where the phone is primarily a content consumption device, tablets, first popularized by the introduction of Apple's iPad in 2010, with their large screens are both content consumption and content creation devices. Their larger screen sizes certainly make it easier to interact with the content found on the Internet and in the apps that enhance the usefulness of the devices. To that end, research has shown that tablet users spend more time with media and entertainment apps than do their smartphone counterparts.[xxxvii] The larger screen size of the tablet allows users to use the device in a manner similar to how they use a personal computer without being tethered to a monitor or as concerned about depletion of power.

You have likely already seen people who have exchanged their five-pound laptop for a pound-and-a-half iPad. This will undoubtedly become more common. Global tablet penetration is expected to practically double from 10.80 percent in 2012 to 20.70 percent in 2014.[xxxviii] Tremendous change is afoot.

The question is, as a marketer, what are the options for you to take advantage of the opportunities presented by the rapid pace of change with smartphones and tablets? That is what I intend to highlight in this section.

As you read what follows, keep in mind that "mobile" should not be thought of as a device, tool, or channel.[xxxix] When thinking about the web, personal computers are not regarded as a channel to be targeted specially. Rather, the goal is to present content that best suits the specifications of the platform. Similarly, mobile should be thought of as a screen with smaller dimensions than a PC but with the advantage of being ever present. Mobile essentially means a more portable way to access content.

Mobile Technology Opportunities

Mobile Apps

Have you ever used a computer without software on it? You probably have. It used to be that almost any computer you purchased had very little functional software on it. The computer was basically a large paperweight until you installed applications that made it useful to you—perhaps Microsoft Word productivity or *Grand Theft Auto* for entertainment. In reality, every computer is only as good as the software that runs on it. That is certainly true for smartphones.

For all that Apple got right with the iPhone by making it easy to use, what made the device super successful is that Apple understood the importance of extending the concept of "easy to use" from the heralded user interface to the phone's ecosystem.

Going against an established software distribution method that said software should be sold by value-added resellers (VARs), Apple decided that software for the iPhone should be sold exclusively on its iTunes App Store. By doing so, they made it easy for developers to sell applications, or apps, they created for the device, and they made it easy for potential buyers to purchase those apps by limiting the ability to buy to one store. This focused approach was just the encouragement third-party developers needed to create applications for what was then a new technology platform. The apps those developers created extended the phone's functionality and allowed it to become a tool for all facets of life rather than just a smarter phone.

Apple's approach has become a model for the industry. Now, each of the major smartphone platforms has a store from which users can buy apps for their phone. While users can take steps to get apps from other places besides these stores, they represent the easiest and safest (i.e., free of viruses or other malicious software) way to procure software for your phone.

Smartphone Platform	Store Name
Apple	iTunes App Store
Android	Google Play
Blackberry	Blackberry App World
Windows	Windows Phone Store

Table 5. Smartphone App Stores

For the marketer, mobile apps can be a powerful way to interact with your audience by seizing upon the "right now" nature of mobile content. In fact, mobile apps should almost be considered the antithesis of the average marketing website. Rather than creating apps that offer access to static information or the exact content available on a website, the mobile app should be engaging and transactional, allowing people to find information that matters to them in the moment.

Which moment, exactly, should you be targeting? That totally depends on the needs of your customers and the goals of your business. Use cases for mobile phone apps are numerous. They include mobile shopping, customer self-service, conference/event information, corporate or marketing, loyalty, and customer education. You may find that any one or a combination of these is useful to your organization.

The Starbucks app found on iOS (Apple) and Android platforms combines use cases into one application. Frequent Starbucks customers often belong to the My Starbucks Rewards (MSR) loyalty program. MSR members have their rewards points increased for each drink or food purchase they make with a Starbucks gift card associated with their account. The Starbucks mobile app allows users to add gift/payment cards to the mobile app on their phone, enabling those users to pay by using their phone rather than the plastic card itself. Additionally, the Starbucks app allows users to manage their accounts, find the locations of nearby coffee shops, and shop for gifts. The app is a great example of giving users information they need right now in a way that facilitates greater engagement with the brand.

Clearly, the Starbucks application is a B2C example, but there are also outstanding opportunities for B2B marketers to take advantage of phone and tablet applications. At a simple level, a chemical manufacturer could create a mobile app that provides access to Material Safety Data Sheets (MSDS) for its products. A more ambitious company might investigate upending an existing offline process so that customers' actions within a product servicing app (e.g., manuals, scheduling repairs, etc.) would integrate with existing sales and marketing systems, providing information on customers' usage and identifying opportunities for upselling and cross-selling. The ability to serve as a real-time resource to your customers can position your company to seize more opportunities for conversion.

A branded mobile app can be a fantastic way to engage your customers. Be mindful, however, that creating a successful mobile app requires a significant commitment in time, money, and personnel. Most successful corporate apps have a well-defined strategy based on achieving a real business goal. Moreover, once the strategy is articulated, a team of developers (likely external to your company) will have to build the app, generally at a cost of $30–70k (or more, depending on its complexity and integration with other systems). Finally, once the app is done and launched, there is a resource intensive effort to measure performance, to identify opportunities for improvement, and to update the app with new versions and/or revised content. You should only commit to building an app when you are sure you are prepared to devote the resources necessary to be successful.

Mobile Sites

Have you ever visited a website on your smartphone and been frustrated by the experience? Issues can range from the site loading slowly to being slowed down by having to zoom in and out to click buttons and read large amounts of text. Users have been forgiving about some of the difficulties they face in accessing standard websites from mobile devices. Mobile dominance, however, will alter website users' willingness to be patient as more and more organizations adapt and begin offering mobile friendly websites.

Mobile dominance on the web is very real. Wireless penetration in the United States is 101 percent[xl]—there are currently more mobile phones activated than there are people in the country. Additionally, in 2012, the smartphone share of the wireless phone market increased to 70 percent. [xli] In other words, seven out of ten mobile phone owners own web-ready smartphones—or, a larger percentage of the population has smartphones than do not. Moreover, depending on your source, between 25 and 30 percent of Americans own tablets, and this number grows each year. Your customers are accessing your website and viewing your e-mails on devices other than PCs. Ignoring this is to risk turning those customers away. A mobile site is an effective way to address this challenge.

The mobile site is designed to accommodate the screen size and functional limitations of the mobile device as compared to the PC. The idea that screen size plays a role in how well people can use your site is an obvious observation. Here are some less apparent challenges people on mobile devices face when it comes to using websites:

- Adobe Flash–Until recently, Flash was ubiquitous. It allowed website owners to display animations and other dynamic content in a way not generally allowed with HTML, the language programmers use to develop websites. Additionally, almost every video viewed on a website has been displayed with the help of Flash. Apple, when launching the iPhone, decided their phone would not support Flash. Other operating systems followed suit. Flash is still used on many corporate sites, but the information displayed by it cannot be seen by most mobile device users.

- Primary Navigation Rollovers–In an effort to make a website easier to navigate, many sites use multilevel navigation menus that allow users to roll their mouse over top-level menu items and see sub-items. This technique is helpful on PCs but very challenging to use on mobile. After all, there is no mouse on mobile and, as a result, it's not simple to roll over menu items. Content that you thought was easy to access is now buried for mobile users.

- Buttons and links–The mouse also benefits PC users in that they can precisely click on links and buttons. Mobile users rely on their fingers to provide device input. Both finger width and obscuring the screen during any given press make it challenging to precisely click a link or button. When the target of the press is isolated, the mobile browser can discern what the user intended to do. When multiple buttons are within close proximity, however, users can mistakenly click the wrong item, resulting in a compromised user experience.

Now that you are aware of some of the challenges users face, how do you go about creating a mobile site? As with most things technology, the ideal solution varies based on your needs and objectives. Rather than tell you what you should do, I will share the most popular options for rendering content that can be easily accessed by users on smartphones and tablets.

The custom mobile site is a common solution for addressing mobile users' needs. It is especially popular with organizations with highly transactional use cases, such as online retailers. Rather than force mobile users to scroll through pages and pages of content intended for PCs, give them a condensed version of the site that only shows what they need. Notice the difference between the versions of two popular sites below.

Target.com Home Page

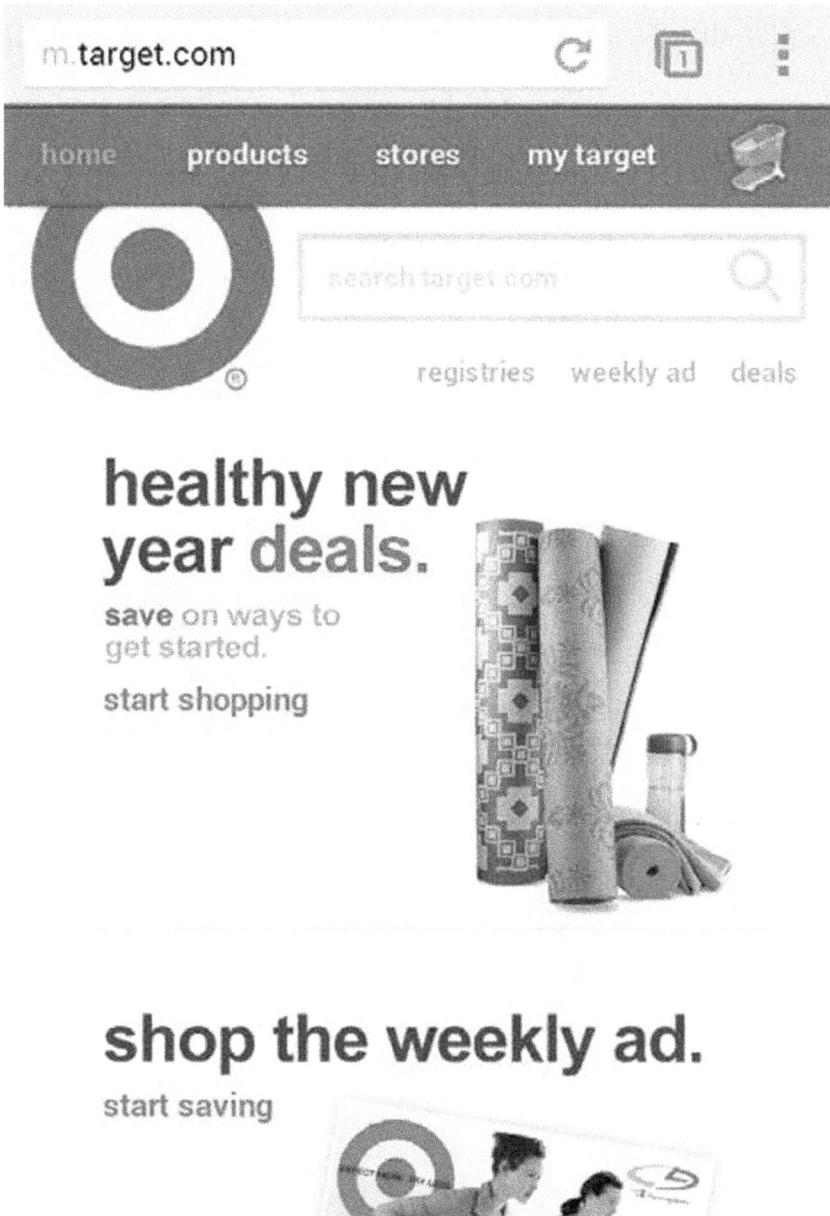

Target.com Mobile Home Page

Notice that Target has condensed the top navigation items from nineteen on the standard home page to four (plus the shopping cart) on the mobile version. They would have decided what to show based on the navigation tabs that were most frequently clicked on the original website. Also important to note is the prominence of the search box on Target's mobile site. Mobile users want to do less clicking than PC-based users. The search box allows them to quickly reach the content they want.

NYTimes.com Home Page

The New York Times

We kept our promise.

Jan 8, 2013, 2:54 PM EST   **Weather** 47°F >   Dow ↓ -73.00 -0.55% >

[   ]   Search   VIEW SECTIONS ▾

TOP NEWS   **Global Edition »**

It's Official: 2012 Was Hottest Year Ever in U.S.

Last year blew away the previous record, set in 1998, by a full degree Fahrenheit.

Under Obama, a Skew Toward Male Appointees

President Obama's second-term inner circle is likely to be dominated by men, and male appointees have outnumbered women in most departments and at all levels of service.

- Aid Groups Report New Level of Misery Among Displaced Syrians

- As Asian-Americans' Numbers Grow, So Does Their Philanthropy

---

NYTimes.com Mobile Home Page

The New York Times' content-heavy home page is converted into a much-reduced version of itself. You will notice the headline on each page is the same, but much of the formatting has been removed. Additionally, the Times has taken the navigation bar and placed it within the "View Sections" link on the mobile version, efficiently using valuable screen real estate.

The mobile site for both Target and the New York Times reformat existing content to better suit the needs of mobile users. Key to sharing content from your existing site with mobile users is having a content management system (CMS) that is able to detect mobile users and present them with a unique user experience. When your CMS is capable of showing different experiences to users based on the type of device they use, you can gain efficiencies because it becomes easier to ensure that the content shown on the standard site matches what appears on mobile, even if *how* it is rendered differs.

Even when the CMS supports reformatting content to be displayed on mobile devices, there is a significant amount of effort necessary to create a useful mobile site. For example, as I pointed out with both Target and the New York Times, both companies chose to alter their primary navigation to better accommodate the mobile platform. Additionally, many companies find that a site structure that works for PCs is not as useful on mobile devices. As a result, they work with their information architects to go beyond altering the primary navigation and endeavor to re-architect the site for mobile users.

Re-architecting the site addresses a few concerns that may otherwise exist. First, creating a new mobile site architecture can result in a mobile site that is easier to browse and search on than might be found on a standard website. Second, often the use cases of mobile users are different from users visiting from a nonmobile browser. Mobile users often want information relevant to a situation based on where they are or what they are doing at the moment. It is frequently less about just browsing than it is getting a piece of information to be used right now. The mobile site, then, can be re-architected to match mobile users' proclivity to want "right now" information.

Although tailoring an interface to make your website more accessible to mobile users while also allowing quick access to "right now" information is a great way to engage your mobile users, it is not the only solution. Many marketers are turning to what is termed "responsive web design" (or just "responsive") to provide a single site that meets the needs of both PC browsers and mobile devices.

Responsive sites use browser technology to adapt to the screen size of the device being used to access the site. For the marketer, rather than having to be concerned with two sites—a standard site and a mobile site—a responsive site allows you to build one site that serves users on PC browsers, tablets, and smartphones. With a site built on responsive design principles, you end up focusing on the maintenance and measurement of one site rather than worrying about determining what should go to the standard site and what should go to the mobile site.

Mobile Site	Responsive Design Site
Pros ✓ Streamlined interface offers easier navigation and access to most important content ✓ Limited content results in faster rendering on mobiles ✓ Inexpensive to build	**Pros** ✓ One site to support multiple types of devices ✓ URLs do not differ between experiences ✓ More effective for search engine optimization and sharing
Cons ✓ Not easily adaptable to multiple screen sizes ✓ Requires building and maintaining multiple sites ✓ Can prove difficult for users looking for standard content ✓ Difficult to track and convert	**Cons** ✓ Challenging to eliminate content not needed on mobile devices ✓ Can be more expensive to build

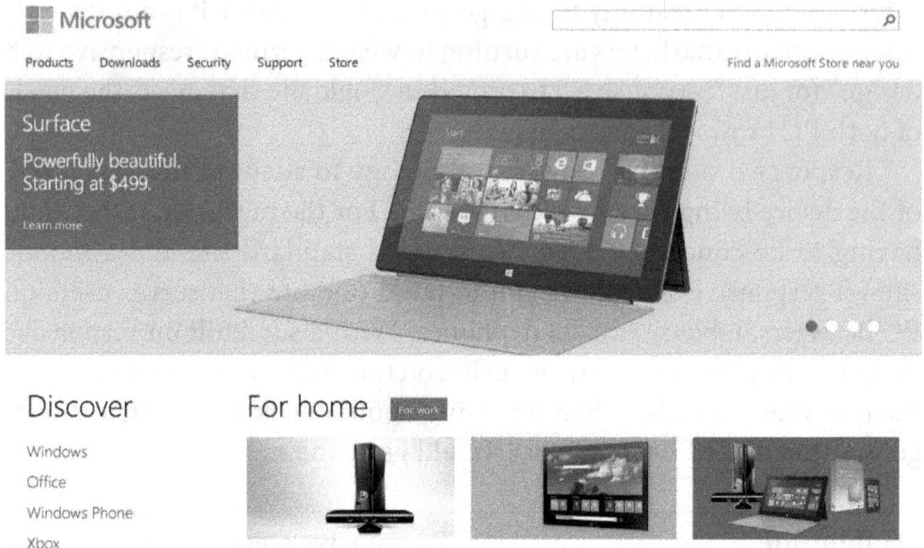

Microsoft.com Home Page—Responsive on PC Browser

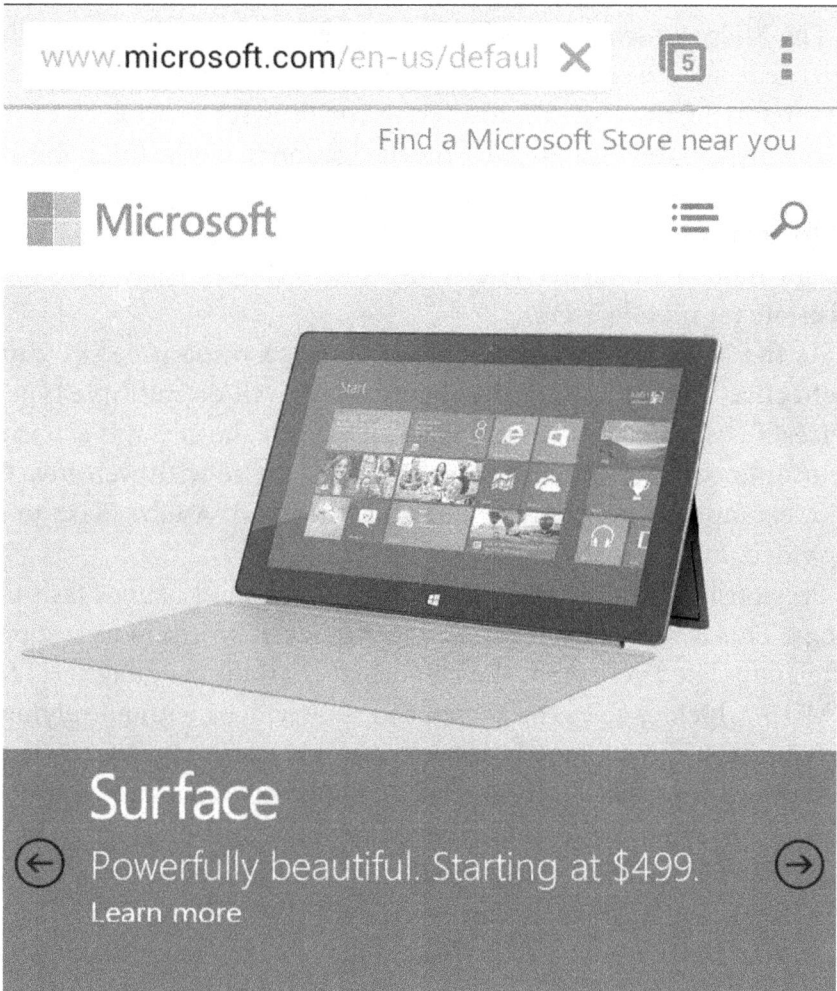

www.**microsoft.com**/en-us/defaul ✕

Find a Microsoft Store near you

Microsoft

Surface
Powerfully beautiful. Starting at $499.
Learn more

Discover

Windows

Microsoft.com Home Page—Responsive on Mobile Browser

The Microsoft.com site is built using responsive web design principles. The result is a site that looks similar regardless of the size of the device supporting the visit. Microsoft relies on browser technology to make two readily apparent differences; the navigation from the full home page has been condensed to a drop-down when viewed by a mobile browser, and the search box from the full site has been hidden behind a search icon for mobile viewers. These changes help the site maximize screen real estate for mobile users.

As the Microsoft example demonstrates, a responsive site can be an effective way to create a site that displays well on multiple types of devices. Because you are building a full website, however, it is possible to run into some of the mobile offenses that arise with websites. One major example, as pointed out earlier, is the use of Adobe Flash to display video.

Previously, showing video on a website required using Flash technology. This is no longer the case. Most modern browsers now support using an updated version of the HyperText Markup Language (HTML), HTML 5, which enables the browser to show videos without relying on Flash. In most cases, the web developer builds the site to detect whether the browser supports Flash and, if so, shows the Flash version of the video. If not, then the HTML 5 video is presented. In most cases, the presentation is seamless and is an effective means of ensuring all of your users have access to your videos.

As you think about whether you want to enable your mobile capability with a dedicated mobile site or with a site that uses responsive web design, keep in mind that neither solution applies to every situation. You may find that for one site—your main site, perhaps—a mobile site is the better solution while on a microsite; your users are better served by a dedicated mobile site. What is right for you and your customers will be best determined on a case-by-case basis.

More important than choosing a solution is making a commitment to serving up content that can be consumed by mobile users. Smartphone use continues to grow in the United States and, in many places worldwide, exceeds the use of desktop and laptop computers for web browsing. Your customers and, even more so, your future customers are using mobile devices, and you need to meet them where they are.

Text Messaging

If you are reading this book, the probability is pretty high that you have already received a text—or more properly, a short message service (SMS)—message. Almost everyone, regardless of whether they have a smartphone or a feature phone, has sent and/or received a text message. It is the ubiquity of the technology that has resulted in over six billion SMS messages being sent daily in the United States alone.[xlii]

For many marketers, there are legitimate reasons to use the prevalence of SMS to your advantage. A staggering 97 percent of text messages are read within three minutes of receipt,[xliii] making text messages effective for short-term, situational marketing such as coupon codes for local shops. Moreover, 50 percent of people who have received a text message have made a purchase as a result of receiving the message, according to a survey.[xliv] Text messages offer a compelling way to engage your customers.

In addition to the text messages you are likely most familiar with, most phones also support multimedia messaging services (MMS) messages. The difference between the much more frequently used SMS messages and MMS messages is that the latter can include images and, in many cases, video. As you can imagine, the ability to add images provides marketers with a lot of flexibility, including being able to brand your messages and move "users through the marketing and purchase process and motivating consumers to act."[xlv] Another difference between SMS and MMS messages is that SMS messages do not rely on a mobile data connection to send and receive the messages. MMS technology, however, usually requires the sender and the recipient to have access to a mobile data connection to exchange those messages. Where almost every cell phone user can send and receive text messages, your MMS messages will be limited to users whose phones support mobile data.

Regardless of whether you choose to use SMS or MMS messages, the approach to actually sending messages is similar:

- **Your customers provide their cell phone number**– Just as with e-mail, opt-in is the best policy for contacting customers by text message, which means asking for the number and confirming the customer is willing to receive messages from your organization. Keep in mind that not all customers have unlimited messaging plans, which could mean a customer could be charged to receive a message from you. Additionally, text messages are an interruptive technology. If you send an unexpected or undesired message to a customer, you risk having the interruption be reason enough to tarnish your brand's perception.

- **Lease common short code (CSC)**–The common short code (usually shortened to "short code") is, in essence, a telephone number that allows you to exchange SMS messages with your customers. They are generally five- to six-digit numbers that are used exclusively for text messages. Procuring a short code requires either applying directly to the Common Short Code Administration (CSCA) or working with a third-party mobile application service provider (MASP) who has already leased a group of short codes from the CSCA.[xlvi]

There are benefits to each option.[xlvii]

	Dedicated	Shared
Pros	• Maintain complete control over short code • Have access to full range of text codes enabling clear calls to action (e.g., "SIGN-UP" vs. "ACME SIGNUP")	• Significantly less expensive • Quick (almost immediate) implementation
Cons	• More expensive than shared ($500–1,000 per month) • Requires working with each mobile carrier to configure • Lengthy timeframe from application to first use (~12 weeks)	• No control over which other brands and companies use "your" short code • Risk not having access to call-to-actions because they're reserved by other organizations

Leasing your own dedicated short code from the CSCA gives you the ability to maintain complete control over your short code. The costs associated with that are as follows: (1) there is greater expense leasing from the CSCA, and (2) you are required to liaise with each individual carrier to ensure your campaign is approved, which can be a time-consuming and laborious process. Leasing your short code from a MASP allows you to get up and running with your short code quickly—immediately in many cases. The risk is, you will likely end up sharing your short code with other companies. It is unlikely, but not impossible, that you and another company could end up advertising the same short code in the same place.

Whether you lease your short code from the CSCA or you lease it from a mobile services vendor, you will be required to pay for the service. The cost for leasing a short code from the CSCA is $500 for a random short code and $1,000 per month for a vanity short code. Because smartphones no longer share number buttons with keys, it is not as useful to purchase a vanity short code as it may have been at one time. With the exception of the most unusual circumstances, you will likely be well served by a random short code.

Leasing a short code from a mobile messaging provider costs substantially less than leasing one from the CSCA. Generally, those organizations charge about $50 per month for the privilege of leasing a shared short code from them.

As mentioned previously, however, you are sharing that short code with other brands.

- Arrange to use short code with third-party messaging provider

- Procuring the short code is just the start. Once you have it, you have to establish a relationship with a third-party messaging provider through which you can exchange messages with your customers. It stands to reason that this is less complicated if you lease your short code through such a service provider. If you lease your short code directly through the CSCA, however, your team must identify a company to handle sending and receiving your text messages.

- Create application or integrate with application that can manage your incoming and outgoing messages

- After setting up your short code, connect it to a system that will properly associate the messages you send and receive with your customers. This can be commercial software like your CRM or e-commerce systems. Or, you can have a third-party system that integrates your short code with a specific marketing system within your organization.

Text messages are a powerful way to engage customers in this phone-dependent society. They are engaging, quick to read, and have numerous use cases with which they can be utilized. The potential complexity in getting them configured for your organization should be outweighed by the impact they can have on your marketing campaigns.

Quick Response (QR) Codes

For a while it looked as if the somewhat weird-looking image in Figure 4, the quick response (QR) code, would play a critical role in helping marketers drive mobile phone users from offline marketing materials to websites on their phones. After all, the point of the QR code is to provide a way for marketers to engage users after they consume a piece of offline content.

The expectation with QR codes is users recognize the image and use the camera on their mobile phone to scan it, at which point the phone implements some engagement action the creator of the image specifies. That engagement typically takes the form of directing the user's mobile browser to a specific URL. QR codes are not limited to containing URLs, though. They can also be used to create text (SMS) messages, dial phone numbers, exchange contact information, and show a text string to the user. In fact, QR codes offer marketers a tremendous amount of flexibility for engaging users who are coming from offline media. That flexibility, however, is countered by some inherent challenges in the technology.

FIGURE 4. QR CODE POINTING TO
WWW.MARKETNOLOGY.COM

Some challenges include the following:

- Limited Awareness of QR Codes: Most consumers are unfamiliar with QR codes. It is estimated that fewer than 10 percent of mobile phone users have scanned QR codes.
- Software is Needed: Most smartphones do not ship with software that allows users to scan QR codes. Rather, the user has to go to the app store associated with her device and download one of many apps that can scan the codes.
- Not Easy to Do: The quality of the phone's camera, the user's ability to hold his hand steady, and even glare from ambient lighting can affect the ease with which codes are scanned. Time and difficulty can turn users off the idea of using QR codes.

In spite of these challenges, many marketers find that the benefits of QR codes outweigh the challenges associated with them. QR codes are free to use and create. Many easily found websites will take information you specify and convert it into a QR code for free. Additionally, the codes do not take up a significant amount space on print materials. As a result, it is simple to place one in whitespace on an existing piece of media or on product packaging. There is no additional cost with placing it, and the code offers you an opportunity to engage customers who are familiar with the technology.

Creating a QR code

If you choose to use a QR code, you will likely be eager to find out they are one of the few technologies that can be created and used without a significant amount of expense. There are numerous websites that will generate a QR code using text information you provide to the site. The code created in figure 4, above, was created for free using that method. That particular code simply takes you to the home page for marketnology.com. There are also more expensive options.

Companies like ScanLife help marketers create QR codes that rely on a customized technology platform enabling more flexibility. Specifically, these platforms allow marketers to gain features like the ability to track the QR codes and, for website codes, change the destination of the code after creation. On top of the technical benefits, in many cases the QR code platforms can help you create branded QR codes that are typically challenging to create with free tools. For the marketer interested in QR codes, options certainly exist to go beyond the standard QR code that links to your website home page.

Mobile Summary

The mobile device as a marketing channel is growing by leaps and bounds. The options presented here for engaging mobile users are just the tipping point. In fact, many of them may have been supplanted by newer, even more exciting technologies by the time you read this. The big takeaway here is that mobile is as important as—and for many marketers, more important than—almost any other channel, including the desktop browser. The time is now for determining how to optimize your users' mobile experiences for engagement, branding, and customer service. Not doing so will put your brand at risk as your competitors will be seizing the moment ahead of them.

---

xxxv. "comScore Reports September 2012 U.S. Mobile Subscriber Market Share," Comscore, November 2, 2012, http://www.comscore.com/Insights/Press_Releases/2012/11/comScore_Reports_September_2012_U.S._Mobile_Subscriber_Market_Share.

xxxvi. Ibid.

xxxvii. "Smartphones Work Round the Clock, Tablets Come Out at Night," Marketing Charts, November 1, 2012, http://www.marketingcharts.com/wp/interactive/smartphones-work-round-the-clock-tablets-come-out-at-night-24442/.

xxxviii. Clearwater Corporate Finance, Global Tablet Penetration Forecast, February 2012, http://www.statista.com/statistics/219909/global-tablet-penetration-forecast/.

xxxix. Christina Kerley, "Mobile Marketing: Three Strategic Approaches to Success," June 12, 2012, http://www.marketingprofs.com/video/2012/8141/mobile-marketing-three-strategic-approaches-to-success-video.

xl. "Wireless Quick Facts," CTIA—The Wireless Association, http://www.ctia.org/advocacy/research/index.cfm/aid/10323.

xli. "NPD Group: Lower Prices and Larger Selection Boost Pre-Paid Mobile Phone Carriers," NPD Group, November 15, 2012, https://www.npd.com/wps/portal/npd/us/news/press-releases/the-npd-group-lower-prices-and-larger-selection-boost-pre-paid-mobile-phone-carriers/.

xlii. Michael O'Grady, "SMS Usage Remains Strong in the US: 6 Billion SMS Messages Are Sent Each Day," June 19, 2012, http://blogs.forrester.com/michael_ogrady/12-06-19-sms_usage_remains_strong_in_the_us_6_billion_sms_messages_are_sent_each_day.

xliii. Greg Stuart, "Mobile Wake Up Call: State of Mobile Today," Mobile Marketing Association, June 2012.

xliv.   "8 in 10 Smartphone Users Have Browsed Products," Marketing Charts, May 27, 2011.

xlv.   Mogreet, "Achieving Tangible ROI with Multimedia Text Message Marketing," September 2012, http://www.mmaglobal.com/research/achieving-tangible-roi-multimedia-text-message-marketing.

xlvi.   Mobile Marketing Association, "Common Short Code Primer," June 2006.

xlvii. Common Short Code Administration, "Shared Versus Dedicated Short Codes."

CHAPTER 9

LEAD GENERATION
AND MARKETING AUTOMATION

At one time, marketers would create a form on a web page and ask site visitors to self-identify as leads and indicate how close they were to making a purchase. In fact, many marketers at companies of various sizes use this tactic and, truthfully, there is nothing inherently wrong with this approach. It does present challenges, however—namely, the marketer relied on the prospect to provide an honest assessment of where she was in the buying process, making it difficult to accurately qualify the lead prior to sending it on to the sales team. Marketing automation attempts to change that process.

Whether they choose to actively identify themselves as leads or not, the passive behavior of visitors to your site can be used to help you understand where they are in the purchasing decision process. For example, people who arrive from search engines and look at a wide range of products are likely to be at the beginning of the purchasing funnel. On the other hand, repeat visits to the same product/service and downloads for a specific product can indicate the user is close to making a decision. Marketing automation software is designed to use both the active and passive information shared by users to help assess their value as a lead.

The technology research firm, Gartner, defines the marketing automation system as "a system that helps marketers execute multi-channel marketing campaigns by providing a scripting environment for authoring business rules and interfaces to a variety of third-party applications."[xlviii] Marketing automation helps B2B marketers create campaigns that drive customers to action and, of critical importance, gets the right leads into the sales pipeline when they are most likely to be ready to purchase.

More specifically, marketers rely on marketing automation to do the following:[xlix]

- Nurture relationships with leads who are not ready to buy–The tools in the marketing automation toolbox contribute to faster growth by companies using marketing automation than those who do not. Moreover, marketing automation users see a greater percentage of the sales pipeline sourced from marketing and stronger revenue plan attainment.

- Retain and extend customer relationships–The behavioral information captured by marketing automation software can result in better understanding of your customers and the delivery of more relevant messaging, positioning you to build more durable relationships with those customers.

- Build sales alignment–Marketing automation gives marketers a system with which the sales team's customer relationship marketing (CRM) system can integrate, resulting in qualified leads being automatically pushed directly to the sales team.

- Prove and improve marketing ROI–Active measurement makes it possible to use the metrics and analysis you attain from the marketing automation system to identify what is and is not working with your campaigns. Strengthening what is working and fixing what is broken generally results in greater sales and higher ROI.

In a study of organizations using marketing automation, it is reported that 60 percent of the surveyed companies improved the quality of leads sent to sales, and 48 percent reported higher quality leads being sent to sales. Furthermore, 28 percent of those companies saw an increase in revenue per sale.[1] Marketing automation can positively impact the success of the marketing efforts in lead-dependent organizations.

The great successes of marketing automation do not come without some effort. As is the case with the implementation of almost any new system, the benefits of marketing automation are more likely to be realized when you develop a plan for implementation that is specific to the needs of your organization. This means going through a marketing automation preparation process that includes fully assessing where you are currently and where you want to end up. The tasks to be performed include the following:

- **Assess team's existing lead management process**–Your existing lead management process offers strong insight into how your organization might handle marketing automation. Companies where the premarketing automation lead management process is organized might have an easier time adapting to the new process than one where the process is held together with sticks and glue. To assess your process, ask yourself the following questions:

  o How are you currently attracting leads?
  o What happens to inbound leads once they arrive at the destination (e.g., landing page, microsite, main website, etc.) you have set for them?
  o How are the leads tracked?

o Are the leads segmented?

o Do you use multitouch programs to engage the leads? What methods do you use to qualify leads?

o What has been the sales team's satisfaction with the leads you send?

- **Understand goals**–It is important to understand why you want to use a marketing automation system. Why do you think it will be valuable to your company? Are you looking for higher return on marketing investment? Is your concern more about delivering more qualified leads? Perhaps you want to automate your existing process with something more modern. Whatever the case, once you have identified your objectives, you should identify key stakeholders within your organization who can help you realize those goals.

- **Engage integration points**–If your organization is like most companies who use marketing automation software, there are multiple teams who participate in the lead management process. Multiple teams may feed the pipeline; multiple sales teams may be served by the process; and your IT team may be responsible for maintaining the existing system. Each team represents an integration point with which you should partner to achieve optimal success.

- **Identify human resource needs**–Members of your team who will have to use the process that results from implementation of the marketing automation system will need to be trained. Quite frankly, they will also need to be willing to adapt to the change in methodologies. As with most software implementations, it is important to identify users who are both most willing to use a new method and can serve as influencers for those who lag behind.

- **Measure success**–This task is related to understanding your goals. Once you have a handle on why you are undertaking this endeavor, you must then determine how you will judge success. This means using your existing lead management metrics as a baseline, establishing benchmarks based on your own expertise and industry best practices, and then setting specific, measurable, attainable, relevant, time-bound (SMART) targets for your organization.

- **Know the Total Cost of Ownership (TCO)**–Be sure to fully understand the costs associated with any marketing automation system you are considering. Know exactly what you want to do on the platform and confirm the pricing associated with each capability with your salesperson and/or integrator. Some platforms give you all available features for a set cost, while other platforms offer add-ons and additional services that can result in much higher costs than anticipated.

Going through these steps will take time, undoubtedly. You will find, however, that the time you take to assess your demand generation needs is time well spent. Taking the time to plan is often the difference between a successful marketing automation implementation and one that experiences lackluster results.

Selecting vendors

Now that you understand your needs and goals, it is time to determine the type of system you need. Truthfully, the platforms offered by many vendors may suit your company's needs. What you want is the system that best integrates into your company's environment in terms of process, user acceptance, and technology.

Look for the following features as you select your system:[li]

- Landing page management
- Website activity tracking
- Personalized microsites
- Lead segmentation
- Lead scoring
- E-mail distributions
- Real-time alerts
- CRM software integration
- Form and survey tools
- Membership management
- Data Hygiene
- Integration with offline marketing
- Marketing analytics

Selecting your system is best done by adhering to a methodology that includes the following steps:[lii]

- *Establish requirements.* Now that you understand your goals, you should be able to determine what features you need in a marketing automation system. You should be as specific as possible based on the type of process you would like to establish. When looking to define your requirements, think more about where you want to be rather than where you are. The requirements themselves can be as specific as, "Allow campaign manager to track real-time performance of second e-mail in a series of four drip marketing e-mails" or "Create business rules to manage the path users take in the lead funnel depending on whether they first came to the site from an prospecting e-mail we sent in January."

- *Research your options.* All systems are not created equally. Each marketing automation system has key differentiators that may make each more or less effective for your company. You have to whittle down the systems in your consideration set to a few reasonable options. Budget and system audience are good ways to initially start clearing the field. Systems designed (and priced) for enterprises may not be right (or affordable) for a medium-sized company. Similarly, a marketing automation platform targeting medium-sized businesses often is not a good fit for even a division of a large company.

- *Put vendors through an exercise.* No amount of research will demonstrate how your company's unique needs will align with a specific platform. For vendors on your refined list, provide them with scenarios you expect to execute with their system and ask them to show you how they would run those scenarios. The scenarios should be fairly complex so you can fully understand how the system would execute multiple steps in the marketing automation process.

- *Talk to references.* Ask the company to provide you with references. The goal with references is not to determine how happy customers are with the system. Rather, you want to know if the references are similar to your own company so that you can be sure the system will serve your organization well.

- *Try it out.* Ask the vendor if you can try the system out in your organization. The best way to determine how well the system fits your organization is to try it out for a limited time. Of course, trying it out requires getting staff on your team trained and, potentially, working with your IT team to get the software installed. That comparatively small investment may be a great risk mitigation strategy against buying a system that is ill-suited for your company.

- *Just do it.* You may have some trepidation about committing. It is a big step. You have come this far, though. Now is the time to commit. This is a big step toward improving the efficiency of your marketing campaigns. It is time to get started.

Marketing Automation Vendors

Company	Web Address	Key Features
Eloqua (Oracle)	www.eloqua.com	Market leader; backing of Oracle; great lead scoring capability; modern, easy-to-use interface; multichannel marketing capability (including mobile and print) with ability to use conditional logic for any step in process; strong training and support; integrates well with Microsoft Dynamics CRM, Siebel, and salesforce.com
Hubspot	www.hubspot.com	Affordable; targets small- and medium-sized businesses but can benefit divisions of larger companies; software as a service (SaaS) reduces dependence on technical staff; many features in addition to lead management capabilities
IBM Marketing Operations	www.ibm.com/ software/market- ing-solutions	Extensive use in financial services, insurance, technology, and communications industries; strong predictive modeling; advanced reporting capabilities; integrates with almost any existing database; part of a larger, very powerful marketing suite

Marketo	www.marketo.com	One of two market leaders; intuitive to use; well-regarded analytics; extensive social media features; powerful modeling functionality; strong integration with salesforce.com; full spectrum of clients across industries and ranging from SMB to enterprises
Neolane	www.neolane.com	Supports multiple types of organizations including B2B, B2B2C, and B2C; offers both on-premises and SaaS options; ability to target segments with dynamic content based on segments; has built-in marketing resource management (MRM) capabilities; supports lead management applications across multiple geographic areas, including support for multiple countries, currencies, languages, and brands[liii]
Pardot (Exact Target)	www.pardot.com	Tightly integrated with ExactTarget's e-mail features; intelligent drip-marketing functionality; "broad" support for search marketing and SEO; built with usability in mind for average marketing user; integrates with salesforce.com and SugarCRM; largely targets SMBs

Silverpop	www.silverpop.com	Extensive e-mail capabilities; easy to use; low cost; ability to post to social media streams and RSS feeds; integrates well with numerous technology providers including Adobe, Microsoft Dynamics CRM, and salesforce.com
Teradata (formerly Aprimo)	www.teradata.com	Mostly deployed in very large organizations; extensive professional services group; advanced features including social media connections; ability to simultaneously use multiple lead scoring models and integration with many CRM platforms[liv]

---

xlviii.   IT Glossary, Gartner, Inc., http://www.gartner.com/it-glossary/mas-marketing-automation-system/.

xlix.   Veronica Maria Jarski, *The Magic Behind the Curtain: Marketing Automation*, March 30, 2013, MarketingProfs, http://www.marketingprofs.com/chirp/2013/10427/the-magic-behind-the-curtain-marketing-automation.

l.   *Marketing Automation Drives B2B Lead Gen Effectiveness*, September 24, 2012, MarketingProfs, http://www.marketingprofs.com/charts/2012/8955/marketing-automation-drives-b2b-lead-gen-effectiveness.

li.   Edy Henao, *How to Select the Right Marketing Automation Software*, CRMSearch.com, http://crmsearch.com/marketing-automation-selection.php.

lii.   *2011 B2B Marketing Automation Vendor Selection Report*, Raab Associates Inc. 2011, http://www.salesleadmgmtassn.com/Articles/RaabVEST_basic_Neolane.pdf.

liii.   Chris Fletcher, *Magic Quadrant for CRM Lead Management*, April 23, 2012, Gartner, Inc.

liv.   *SiriusView: Marketing Automation Platforms*, SiriusDecisions, 2012.

CHAPTER 10

WEB CONTENT MANAGEMENT AND DIGITAL EXPERIENCE MANAGEMENT

At the risk of generating mass hysteria, I am going to make a blanket statement. Of the numerous customer experience management technologies available to marketers, the web content management system (referred to frequently as both WCM and CMS) is the most important tool the marketer has. It is the foundation for properly managing users' digital experiences.

The user experience should be at the core of everything you present to your customers and prospects on the web (and offline, too, honestly). Your customers will judge your brand by the complete range of the experiences they have with it. The content management system is there to enable marketers to deliver a consistent digital experience to users on multiple devices across the full range of the sites you may have.

The CMS is not a new technology. Marketers and IT teams have relied on them almost since corporations decided they should have websites. In the early years, they made it easier for business (marketing and communications, especially) teams to manage web pages for desktop browsers without relying on the cost or timing associated with having technology staff update the HTML code associated with the pages. Additionally, CMSs facilitated workflows that permitted a multilevel review process designed to ensure content that made it to the live site was approved by the company's legal team and the site editor. Things have changed dramatically since those days.

While the CMS is still used to maintain content integrity on the live site and minimize the IT effort associated with deploying content, it has also assumed other roles. The combination of those roles—almost all focused on delivering an exceptional experience—have resulted in CMSs now being referred to in many quarters as customer experience management (CXM) or digital experience management platforms rather than the familiar CMS of yore.

Essentially, the CXM platform integrates many of the very technologies I have already covered into one platform, endowing marketers with a more holistic way to manage the user experience. Forrester describes the systems as allowing "businesses to create and manage digital content, engage with customers across digital customer touchpoints, and measure cross-channel engagement...through technologies such as: content management, commerce, targeting, analytics, and optimization."[lv]

In essence, the combination of these features acknowledges that enabling rich customer experiences online is about more than just presenting any content. Rather, it involves delivering the right content to the right user at the right time on the right (preferred) touchpoint—and it is better for the marketer if those "rights" can be managed with one software system—limiting complexity and minimizing the learning curve so the marketing team can focus on getting things done.

Unfortunately, it is much more difficult for the marketer to act on the "rights" in practice than it is for me to write about it in theory. While some vendors are moving toward delivering robust tools that fully enable management of the customer experience, most do not have the ability to deliver on the concept. As a result, different companies are at different places on the content management versus CXM spectrum. Much of the reason for this is the feature set marketers need to adequately engage customers.

These features comprise what I refer to as the 3Ms: Motivate, Measure, and Manage. The 3Ms (see Figure 5 below) are part of a continuous improvement cycle allowing marketers to improve their performance over time.

3Ms of Customer Experience Management

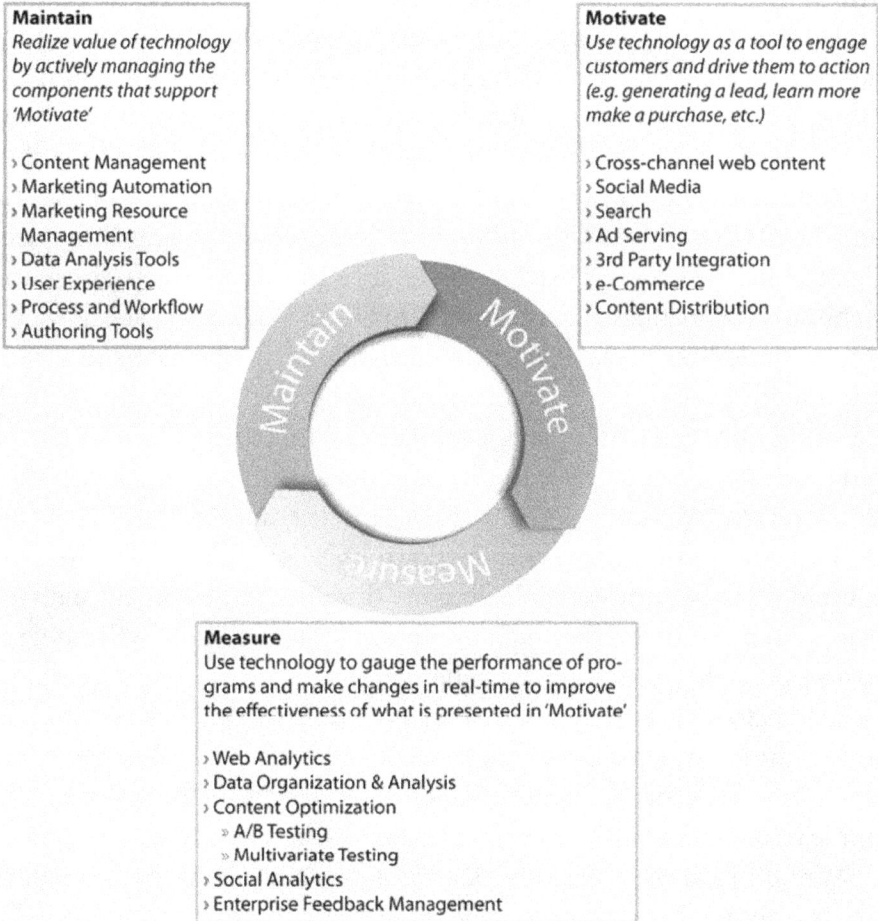

Maintain
Realize value of technology by actively managing the components that support 'Motivate'

> Content Management
> Marketing Automation
> Marketing Resource Management
> Data Analysis Tools
> User Experience
> Process and Workflow
> Authoring Tools

Motivate
Use technology as a tool to engage customers and drive them to action (e.g. generating a lead, learn more make a purchase, etc.)

> Cross-channel web content
> Social Media
> Search
> Ad Serving
> 3rd Party Integration
> e-Commerce
> Content Distribution

Measure
Use technology to gauge the performance of programs and make changes in real-time to improve the effectiveness of what is presented in 'Motivate'

> Web Analytics
> Data Organization & Analysis
> Content Optimization
  » A/B Testing
  » Multivariate Testing
> Social Analytics
> Enterprise Feedback Management

FIGURE 5. 3Ms CUSTOMER EXPERIENCE MANAGEMENT

Because the CMS generally drives what your customers see when they interact with any digital touchpoint of your organization, it plays a role in each of the 3Ms. As the system that presents content to your customers, the CMS is critical to the "Motivate" phase. After all, that phase is all about encouraging people to engage with your company through some action (e.g., read more, generate lead, buy something, etc.) that brings them closer to a deeper relationship with you. Search, social, and display ads often lead back to the sites and/or microsites presented by the CMS. Moreover, the CMS frequently integrates with an e-commerce system to support sales and/or a third-party entity to distribute content.

The tools used within the "Measure" component of the cycle must integrate with the CMS to be effective. The web analytics system ties into the CMS so that the individual pages users view and links users click can be tracked and used to make decisions about the performance of the site. Additionally, content optimization software that allows you to test content by presenting different content to alternate site visitors also integrates with the content management system. Finally, the website, and hence the CMS, plays a critical role in getting users to provide feedback into the enterprise feedback management system. Successfully executing the "Measure" phase requires integration with the CMS.

The "Maintain" phase is similarly strongly dependent upon the CMS. Content refreshes, for example, happen directly in the content management system. Your marketing automation system usually will integrate with your CMS to monitor lead behavior and present the right content to the site visitor. Data analysis software provides insights that inform your content and marketing program decisions by including CMS behavioral data as a source for its analysis. As an interface to customers and a key source of data, the CMS is a critical component of the Maintain phase.

While I refer to each of the 3Ms as a distinct phase, that nomenclature is only for ease of conveying an idea. In practice, each "phase" is actually an equal-sized piece of the foundation of the digital experience you deliver to your clients. Modern marketing dictates that simply presenting content is not enough. The performance of that content must be measured, and the systems associated with delivering that content should be updated regularly to optimize the ability of that content to engage customers and get them to perform the actions that increase your KPIs.

Choosing the Content Management System

Given the role of the content management system as a linchpin of your digital customer experience management efforts, it is clear that choosing the CMS is one of the most important decisions a marketer will make. After all, it is likely that each website you develop will be hosted by the CMS, and almost every other CXM system you acquire will integrate with the CMS.

There are lots of criteria people use to assess how any given CMS will suit an organization. Usually, those criteria are based on the features and functionality offered by the software. For example, does one CMS provide better workflow management than another? While features and functionality are important, the truth is, it is almost impossible to know what features and functionality your organization needs without first understanding your organization's total content management needs.

I will not lecture you on the benefits of assessing your department's or company's situation before endeavoring on the purchase and implementation of a large system like a CMS (or any system, for that matter). After all, I do that elsewhere in the book. What I believe is important, however, is sharing a framework you can use to increase the likelihood that you are considering the CMS features and functionality that are right for your stakeholders—your team, your organization, and your customers.

Addressing the needs of each of those constituent groups means thinking more strategically about the CMS than just the features of the system. Instead, the conversation should be about what you and stakeholders want to achieve. To that end, the framework requires serious deliberation (and answers) about the following points:[lvi]

- **The Strategic Plan**–If your organization already has an up-to-date strategic digital plan, then you should use it as a guide for matching your company's long-term strategic goals with the CMS offerings in the marketplace. Moreover, the strategic plan should allow you to articulate how you define success for web content management and for the entire digital customer experience.

  If your organization does not have a modern strategic digital plan, then that should be your priority. A strong digital plan is the organization's blueprint for building a digital infrastructure and supporting digital platforms. The absence of one increases the risk that multiple departments and teams will duplicate efforts as each attempts to respond to market pressures with a solution that benefits only the individual group. Such efforts result in significant difficulty when the plan is eventually created and all legacy systems are migrated into one or two systems—as they should have been originally.

- **The Optimized Experience**–Because the WCM system you select will likely serve you for years to come, it is important that you and your team think about the types of experiences your customers expect and what will encourage them to be engaged by and interact with the brand. Doing this requires a combination of understanding existing engagement options and looking through a crystal ball to determine what might be coming. The future casting is not supposed to be perfect. Rather, you go through the process to be better able to determine the flexibility of your CMS. Ideally, you want a system that can accommodate both the demands of today's customers as well as their expectations as technology changes and new opportunities for engaging them arise.

- **Implementation Cost**–In this case, the term "cost" does not apply exclusively to monetary value. Rather, the costs associated with implementation of a CMS are spread across the organization. If hosting the software internally, your IT team will be responsible for installing the software and ensuring the security and uptime of the servers on which the software runs. Moreover, agency partners may have to learn how to use the software and may need access to develop licenses from your vendor to build websites that support the CMS. In addition to those costs, there are also expenses associated with maintaining numerous multichannel websites for multiple groups. Someone has to manage and maintain those sites. It is necessary to understand how those costs impact the organization, the marketing team, and customers' digital experiences.

Once you have a clearer understanding about the strategic digital goals of the organization, you can align those needs with the tactical ones (e.g., support multiple sites) that drive feature and functionality expectations. The most common features decision makers use to choose content management systems include the following:[lvii]

- **Multisite**–Many enterprise organizations host numerous websites. There is the primary.com and perhaps distinct sites for divisions or for specific brands. Additionally, marketers frequently launch disparate microsites for individual campaigns. For organizations where all of these sites are managed by one entity (e.g., e-business, IT, etc.), there is a need for the CMS to support hosting multiple sites with different domains within one system.

- **Localization**–With a large percentage of many global organizations' revenues originating outside the United States, it is important that content written in English be available in other languages. Localization enables that by storing multiple versions of content in different languages and associating those versions with relevant copy blocks so that the site can present region specific information without making significant changes to the design of the site.

- **Editing and Design**–Even if your IT team is responsible for uploading an initial batch of content upon implementation of the CMS, it is likely the marketing team will be tasked with updating and maintaining existing content and, when necessary, creating additional content. As a result, it is important to prioritize the ease of use associated with creating and editing content. Some CMS providers feature functionality over ease of use and others just the opposite. For most marketers, it is important to find a package that balances feature set with a user interface that allows practitioners to edit content without being cumbersome and/or requiring lots of steps.

- **Metadata**–Finding content on the web without access to a search engine like Google or Bing would be almost impossible. As websites grow, it is similarly difficult to find content. Even a relatively small 150-page site can prove challenging to manage without an ability to quickly find the pages you seek. The ability to assign metadata to the content living within your site allows you to organize the site by standard groupings that make it easier not just to find content but also to determine where content should be made available within the site. Moreover, some CMSs are able to use metadata to limit access to content based on business rules applied within the metadata.[lviii] This is an important feature and worthy of consideration.

- **Ease of Use**–I already touched on this above in Editing and Design, but it is worth reiterating. Modern CMSs are very robust and powerful applications. Their out-of-the-box capabilities are substantial, and many can be extended with even greater features. The consequence of this robustness is software developers are tasked with adding access to these features into a user interface that is limited. Some companies do a better job of this than others. If marketing is going to be responsible for managing content on the site, ease of use will drive success of the CMS implementation. If the team (with appropriate training) is able to easily create and update content within the site without significant disruption to their existing processes, they will be more likely to use the system.

- **Workflow Management**–From both a credibility and legal perspective, validating the content that reaches the website is a high priority for most organizations. Workflows give teams the ability to have content updates go through a series of approvals before actually being promoted to the public page. Each approval is noted and tracked within the system. As an example, a marketing intern might update a paragraph on a page within the site. With workflow management, a process can be designed, necessitating the update to go through approvals from the intern's boss, a VP, a legal department member, and then corporate communications before being posted to the page. This process limits the company's exposure associated with errors or even sabotage from disgruntled employees. Most WCM applications have workflow management, but the capabilities of each system will differ.

- **System Integration**–In today's technology-driven marketing world, the CMS almost never lives in a silo. Any number of different third-party systems may need to integrate with the CMS. Because the CMS is the interface to users, many of the very systems I have covered integrate with the system, including marketing automation, analytics and optimization, enterprise feedback management, and so on. Additionally, integration points outside your organization might include advertising networks and content licensees who may require support for programmatic interfaces via application programming interfaces (APIs). Anticipating the integration points for which you should be prepared is much easier when you start your content management selection process after the organization has gone through a long-term digital strategy assessment.

- **Customer Support**–This is the most important criterion associated with selecting any content management system. There must be an organization in place that can support your team during implementation and usage of the software. It is preferable for this organization to be a professional services organization within the company that sells the software. This company should know the software better than anyone else and should be best able to provide you with the know-how you need to successfully overcome issues that arise during implementation and usage.

The priorities of each criterion will vary from company to company. Organizations with lots of content may value metadata over ease-of-use because of the importance of organizing that content into easily searchable chunks. Consequently, I am unable at this juncture to specify which criteria should be most important to you and your team. Such a decision should be based on the culture of your organization and the goals of both your group and the overall company. Once you have decided which criteria are most important to you, you can begin reviewing vendors.

Vendors

There are many different content management systems—some good, some not so good. Some that are commonly regarded as good are not suitable for large environments, and others commonly thought to be bad are exactly what is needed for a specific situation (though that is rare).

The content management systems below are commonly thought to be strong performers and are generally well regarded. I am taking care to separate the list into free, open-source software and enterprise software. The free, open-source software options are very good applications and might be just right for your company or your division. Drupal, for example, runs the whitehouse.gov website and is used by *The Economist* magazine and many Fortune 500 companies like Johnson & Johnson.

On the other hand, you may find that commercial options have more features out of the box, whereas open-source options often require modules/extensions (add-on software used to add or enhance functionality) to get many features. You may also find that your technology team is responsible for greater support and training with open-source software as those services can be limited when compared to the professional service offerings of many enterprise content management system options.

Open Source Content Management Systems

Company *Product*	Web Address	Key Features
Alfresco Software *Alfresco*	www.alfresco.com	Supported by a commercial company, Alfresco; offers both free version and more stable and better supported paid version; has built-in mobile and social sharing support; well regarded for document management and collaboration capabilities
Acquia *Drupal*	www.drupal.org	Supported by a commercial company, Acquia; strong enterprise presence; native support for multiple sites; large community of knowledgeable developers
Automattic *Wordpress*	www.wordpress.org	Supported by commercial company, Automattic; popular in publishing community; strong, flexible blogging platform; native support for multiple sites; large community of knowledgeable developers

Commercial Content Management Systems

Company *Product*	Web Address	Key Features
Adobe *Adobe* *Experience* *Manager*	www.adobe.com	Intuitive user experience and natural integration with Adobe-owned tools like Analytics and Target; strong relationships with tech integration partners; focus on marketers' needs
Ektron *Ektron 9*	www.ektron.com	Supports multichannel experiences out of the box; powerful search facility; combination of developer, webmaster, and marketer focus makes it great for informational and marketing sites
HP **Autonomy** *LiveSite/* *TeamSite*	www.autonomy.com	Large legacy installed base as Interwoven Teamsite means ample support available; powerful built-in personalization; social integration; robust partner ecosystem and global support
IBM *Web Content* *Manager 8.0*	www.ibm.com	Tightening integration with IBM's other enterprise marketing and e-commerce products; addresses needs of both marketers and IT teams; supported by IBM's global reach

OpenText *Web Experience Management*	www.opentext.com	Legacy installed base as Vignette CMS; powerful personalization offers granular content targeting
Oracle *WebCenter Sites*	www.oracle.com	Strong support for mobile sites and video; integrates well with third-party systems; well-thought-of personalization engine; has complementary role with Oracle's data analysis and marketing tools
SDL *SDL Tridion*	www.sdl.com	Global reach and very capable localization feature set; focused on digital marketing and e-commerce solutions; SDL has portfolio of complementary products
Sitecore *Sitecore 7*	www.sitecore.net	Well integrated, one-stop-solution shop for digital customer experience management; competitively priced, including TCO; offers functionality to test site UI on multiple devices across multiple channels

There are no perfect WCM solutions. Each excels in some ways but is lax in others. The options presented here are no exception. They do, however, represent the best of the most highly considered options for enterprise marketers.

When the time comes for you to consider a WCM system, I would encourage you to consider these options and to identify other solutions that might be appropriate for you. There are many in the marketplace.

You may find, for example, that rather than relying on one solution, your ideal option uses a commercial enterprise solution for corporate communications and an open-source system for marketing sites. It is impossible to know what product best meets the challenges of your environment without first doing due diligence to understand both your short-term and long-term needs.

lv.   "Climbing the Digital Experience Maturity Ladder Through an Integrated Technology Approach," August 2012, Forrester Research, Inc.

lvi.   David Aponovich, "Fire, Ready, Aim! How Not to Choose a New Web Content Management Solution," http://blogs.forrester.com/david_aponovich/13-05-07-fire_ready_aim_how_not_to_choose_a_new_web_content_management_solution, May 7, 2013.

lvii.   Mick MacComascaigh, Mark R. Gilbert, Gavin Tay, and Jim Murphy, "Magic Quadrant for Web Content Management," September 6, 2012, Gartner, Inc.

lviii.   Troy Allen, "The Importance of Metadata in Content Management," January 10, 2011, http://www.cmswire.com/cms/enterprise-cms/the-importance-of-metadata-in-content-management-009746.php.

PART III

MARKETING AND TECHNOLOGY: PERFECT TOGETHER

CHAPTER 11

CHOOSING YOUR WEAPONS

Making Effective Marketing Technology Decisions

L et us take a moment to distinguish the types of technology options available to marketers. Specifically, I want to address the issue of open source versus commercial off the shelf (COTS) versus software as a service (SaaS).

Term	Explanation
Commercial off the shelf (COTS)	Purchased by most enterprises, COTS software includes products from any manufacturer who sells products for which licenses are provided in exchange for payment. Generally, COTS software is installed in the environment for which the license has been procured. Software from both large vendors like Microsoft and smaller vendors like the creators of mobile phone apps are considered COTS products.

Open source	Especially popular with the growth of the Internet, open-source software includes a license that specifies that, generally, the software is offered for free even for commercial use. The open-source license allows people who use the software to modify and extend the original "source code" of the application to meet their own needs—without owing any payment to the original application creator. Among the most popular open-source applications are the browser Mozilla Firefox and the database program that powers a significant portion of the Internet, MySQL.
Software as a service (SaaS)	SaaS software is fully enabled by the Internet. Rather than having organizations rely on their IT departments to install, configure, and maintain software, SaaS software is hosted in "the cloud" by the company that creates the software. There is nothing to install, no hardware to purchase, and no infrastructure to manage. Each organization interested in using the software only has to purchase a license and direct individuals, most often, to a website through which access is provided. License payment usually occurs on a recurring basis either monthly or yearly. SaaS products with which you may be familiar include Gmail and Salesforce.com.

Table 6. Commercial Software Types

Software is clearly necessary for modern marketing. Selecting the software option that delivers the most value for your organization requires full information about what is available. As described in the table above, you will likely have multiple types of software to consider as you assess what you need to achieve your business requirements. So, how do you decide which offers the best option for you?

Truthfully, there is no easy answer to this question. What works well for one marketing department may not be as effective for a comparably staffed group at a similar company. Your needs may differ because of the way your team is configured or as a result of the pace at which you execute campaigns. Additionally, factors outside your marketing purview, such as the availability of technology department staff and the ability of your IT department to install and host the software you purchase, will affect your decision.

Selecting the right software is a three-step process:

1. Understanding the criteria that will impact your decision
2. Assessing your needs and comparing them to those factors
3. Reviewing the software options that are available to you based on your needs assessment

Understanding decision criteria

Any information technologist will tell you that there are numerous factors that can impact the type of software you choose. There are a few, however, that invariably apply to situations in which someone has to determine how to optimally service their operational needs with software. They are as follows:

- **Time to market**–What is the timeframe in which you want to get to market? Commercial software can often result in getting to market quickly because it comes with a base configuration and is ready to go. Open Source software, on the other hand, often requires software customizations that can extend the time it takes to deploy it in the field. With some minor branding customizations, most SaaS software allows companies to get to market immediately as the software, as a result, cannot be customized and is offered as is.

> *CAVEAT: I HAVE WORKED WITH CLIENTS WHO HAVE LICENSED SaaS PLATFORMS THAT, THOUGH BUILT TO OFFER A ONE-SIZE-FITS-ALL SOLUTION, HAVE PAID ADDITIONAL FEES TO HAVE THE PLATFORM DEVELOPERS CUSTOMIZE THE PLATFORM TO THEIR NEEDS. THIS ARRANGEMENT, THOUGH IT ADDS SIGNIFICANTLY TO TIME-TO-MARKET REQUIREMENTS, CAN BE BENEFICIAL TO YOU BECAUSE IT ALLOWS YOU TO TAKE ADVANTAGE OF THE CORE COMPETENCY OF A VENDOR WHILE LIMITING YOUR EXPOSURE TO RISKS ASSOCIATED WITH HAVING YOUR IT DEPARTMENT INSTALL, CONFIGURE, AND SUPPORT A NEW SOFTWARE APPLICATION.*

- **Budget**–How much money do you have? If you choose open source or commercial software, it is possible your information technology department will bill your department for the resources it expends to maintain that software. This is over and above the cost for licensing the application and paying the professional service fees of the software's manufacturer or an integrator. These costs add up quickly, and while you may be fine with the expense, it is important to understand them at the outset rather than to be surprised down the road.

- **Maintenance**–Does your team or your company have resources that can be trained to support the software and ensure that it is available for use by your team? The software license is the easy part of buying any software. Once you have the software, someone has to maintain both the hardware systems on which the software is reliant and the software itself. For example, the software manufacturer may release security or functionality updates that are critical to continued use of the product, or application data may become corrupted. Both of these scenarios necessitate that someone be knowledgeable about managing the application. This person must be identified prior to licensing the software as his or her absence may indicate this software is not a good investment for you at this time.

- **Customization**–Can this software be used to successfully achieve your goals right "out of the box?" Most software requires some customization. Perhaps it is only that your data have to be entered into the software's database so that calculations can be performed. On the other hand, it may be that significant customizations are required to integrate the application with other systems in your enterprise environment. Whatever the case, it behooves you to be aware of the customizations necessary to make software work in your environment. Underestimating important customizations can significantly alter your implementation schedule and result in decreased ROI.

- **Organization security preferences**–What type of security guidelines has your organization set in place for company-owned data? One of the benefits of SaaS products is that they are not dependent upon your company's technology infrastructure and human resources, which has the potential to be problematic for some organizations, however, where data security guidelines specify that customers' personally identifiable information (PII) and other sensitive company data cannot be shared with systems outside the enterprise's technical infrastructure. At most companies, exceptions can be made where sufficient measures are in place to protect the security of the data. The exact measures will come from your company's data security team, and you should check with them to determine what is necessary. In most cases, they will require that the vendor you select adhere to specific data exchange security policies that may result in additional licensing fees over those quoted for standard instances of SaaS software.

- **Support**–Are there human resources (internally or externally) upon whom you can rely to manage the software or perform required customizations? Any given software is used more or less commonly than its competitors. The number of people familiar with any piece of software and available to help you manage or customize that software is generally directly proportional to the popularity of the software. Commonly used products have lots of people available with the skills to adroitly manage the application. Conversely, less usage means fewer and, thanks to the law of supply and demand, more expensive resources to help you. The cost of purchasing an obscure, low-cost product that matches your needs exactly may end up proving more costly than buying a more expensive product for which there are many knowledgeable people available to help you customize it.

- **Training**–How will your staff learn how to use the software? Often the manufacturers of commercial software provide either on-site training where your staff can learn to use the software you purchase, or they offer off-site training sessions where your staff can also learn tips and tricks from other companies using the same software. Where training is not available from the creator of the application, as will likely be the case for SaaS and open-source software, there may be third parties who offer off-site training sessions your staff can attend. In the worst case, you will end hoping the user interface of the software you select is intuitive enough for your staff to become acclimated simply by using it frequently. This, however, is not a good option, and to encourage the success of any new software, proper training is recommended upon its introduction to new users.

- **Documentation**–How will your staff's questions about the product be answered once the software is installed and training is over? Many manufacturers offer organizations the option to purchase call-center support. This option can be expensive, however. Well-written and well-organized documentation can arm your users with answers to the questions they have about the software without relying upon a manufacturer's call center. It is important to get an idea about the quality of the available documentation prior to committing to purchasing software as poor quality documentation can impact the user acceptance of new software. Should you be set on purchasing software that does not have strong documentation, it may be worth engaging a technical writer who can go through the software and write documentation specific to your organization.

- **Hosting infrastructure**–Can the environment in which you plan to install the software handle your needs? Mission-critical software will have more substantive hosting needs than will applications used occasionally by small groups of users. If you are installing high-priority software, then you should ensure your information technology team is capable of maintaining a high availability server environment where someone is available around the clock to address issues. If that isn't the case, but you are sure you have a need for this critical software, you may want to explore hosting in a managed hosting environment outside your organization, or using a SaaS option.

- **Your requirements**–I intentionally saved the most important criteria for last. Why do you need this software, and what will it allow you to do? One of the biggest mistakes people make when choosing new software is choosing the wrong application. Perhaps they go with the option that has the most positive word-of-mouth, or maybe they select the first vendor they come across rather than doing due diligence and assessing the strengths and weaknesses of the various options that exist. Whatever the case, if the capabilities of the software you choose do not match your own requirements, the software will likely fail. Avoiding this means having a solid grasp on the requirements of your organization at both a senior, strategic level as well as a junior, more tactical level. After all, for most software, it is the junior-level people who administer and use it most often, entering data and generating reports for senior-level managers and executives.

Successfully choosing software will require you and your staff to decide on the priorities of each of these factors for your project and then to weigh potential service providers against those priorities. There are cases where competitive pressures necessitate that short time to market may have a higher priority than the availability of strong documentation or the ability to make customizations. These priorities must be determined on a case-by-case basis.

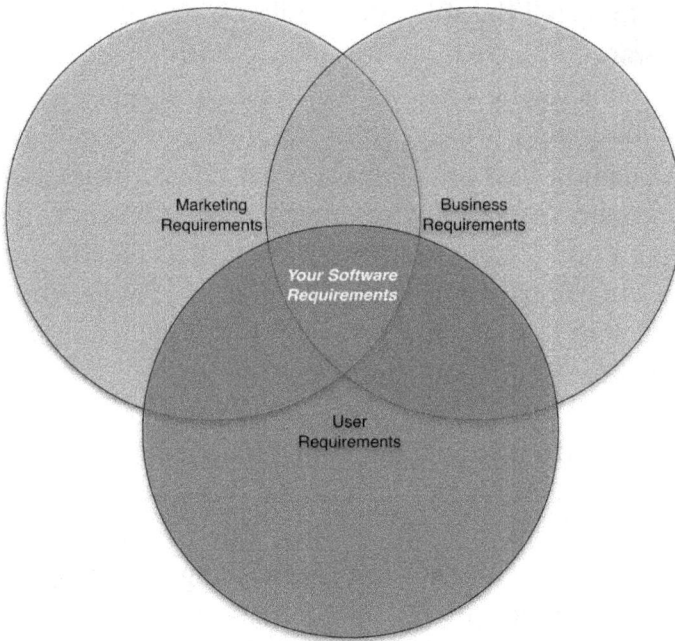

FIGURE 6. SOFTWARE REQUIREMENTS VENN DIAGRAM

The factor that should almost always have the highest priority, however, is your requirements. Accurately assessing your requirements calls for a firm understanding of your marketing needs, the needs of the business, and the needs of your users.

Defining your requirements

Remember back in grade school how your world changed when you moved from number-based problems to math word problems? Success with those problems greatly depended on your ability to understand the story that was told. What most of us did not realize in grade school is that most of life is one big word problem. The clearer the story that is told, the simpler it is for us to understand it, and the easier it is to design a solution to solve the problem.

The idea of the clear and comprehendible story is key in a world where you, the marketer, are not just developing marketing programs but are increasingly building marketing solutions that rely on technology. For marketers, your codified requirements end up being the story that determines the ultimate solution.

How do you go about assessing your requirements and assembling them in a way that results in a successful marketing solution? That's the million-dollar question and, truthfully, there is no right answer. Some marketers rely on the marketing requirements documents (MRD) to organize their information and deliver a well-thought-out approach to their requirements. Others rely on a similar document, the product requirements document (PRD), to deliver their requirements. Other marketers are taking a relatively new approach that relies on the concept of personas (detailed narratives developed about fictional individuals whose behaviors represent a member of the marketer's target audience) and the challenges faced by the users/customers represented by those personas. The "right" approach differs from team to team and company to company.

The right approach for me has ended up being a custom one that I originally created as a document designed to succinctly explain my clients' problems. Over the years, it has grown to include more information and, as a result, is much less concise. What it loses in brevity, however, it gains in clarity and effectiveness.

I use what I call the STAIR document. The acronym is based on the idea that each new project is intended to take us higher (i.e., improve performance, lead to more customers, make us look good, etc.). (Eternal optimism means we'll ignore the idea that stairs can also take us lower.) The letters in the acronym stand for Situation, Timeframe, Audience, Implementation, and Result. When done well, these five themes can be combined to help us answer the *who, what, when, where, why* and *how* of almost any project and tell a story that leads to a successful solution. Below, I describe the purpose and contents of each section of the document:

Section	Description
Situation	**Goal:** Explain the purpose of the project and detail why it's needed. **Approach:** Begin with an explanation of the current situation—answering the questions "Why do we need this project?" and "What are the driving factors for this project?" Consider the following factors: - Business expectations - Customer/prospect goals and expectations - Competitive pressures Two to three specific challenges to be solved should be identified. Once completed, a third party should be able to read about your situation and grasp the reasons for pursuing this project.

Timeframe	**Goal:** Specify the timing associated with the project. **Approach:** There are multiple time elements associated with any marketing project. The most obvious of these is the time to market. Along with this, there should be some description about what is driving the timing. For example, is there a seasonal driver (e.g., an annual holiday, a yearly conference, etc.), a competitive pressure (e.g., a big competitor launches a new product on "x" date), or a business impetus (e.g., the sales team begins a renewed push to sell an existing product) that impacts the time to market? In addition to time to market, there are other time considerations that should be detailed here: ▪ Phases–Does the timing necessitate phasing some project elements so they get into market earlier than others? How are the phases delineated? ▪ Time in market–How long is it expected that the project deliverable would be in market? What is driving that timing? Upon completion, the reader should have a complete picture of the amount of time allowed to develop the assets associated with the project and get them deployed. Additionally, understanding phasing and time in market arms the reader to make well-informed decisions about resource utilization.

Audience	**Goal:** Provide definition around the audience(s) to whom the project is targeted. **Approach:** One of the best ways to address this section is to simply list the audience(s) you want to reach with this project. Then, begin to answer the following questions: - Why is this audience the right target for this project? - Why would this audience want to be on the receiving end of this marketing program? - Can the audience be segmented (or is it already segmented) to allow more targeted marketing? - Are there specific behavioral or technical proclivities we should be aware of regarding this audience that may impact the development of this program (e.g., a large percentage of them are blind, or many will access the program on mobile devices, etc.)? Once the details have been provided for each target, prove the details with personas for each target audience. By using personas to prove the details, you increase the likelihood of developing a program based on the actual behavior of your audience rather than relying on your assumptions about their behaviors. A completed audience section will provide enough information for the reader to feel as if she could answer the following question: *Do I know enough about the audience(s) to successfully execute this project without asking for any more details about the targets?*

Implementation	**Goal:** Detail the tactics that will be used to execute the project. **Approach:** This is the last section of the STAIR to be completed. After all, the tactical approach taken to solve the challenges is totally dependent upon the strategy as defined by each of the STAIR components of the document. This section should be seen as a living, breathing facet of this document. It is likely that you will not detail the entire solution to your challenges on your first pass at Implementation. In fact, that should not be your goal. Rather, your initial objective should be to identify the marketing channels you and your team believe would best allow you to achieve your goals as specified in the other parts of the STAIR. There is no easy way to address this section. It requires hard work. After all, it will dictate how your budget is spent and your human resources are used throughout the project's execution. For each tactic, ask yourself the following questions: <ul><li>Is this tactic quantitatively measurable?</li><li>Will this tactic help us achieve the metrics specified in the Results section of the STAIR?</li><li>Is there at least one member of the Audience specified in the STAIR who is known to respond well to this tactic?</li><li>Does my team have the expertise to use this tactic well? If not, can I find resources to help me do it well?</li></ul>

- Will the ROI on the tactic be sufficiently positive?

Answering negatively to any of the above questions should give you pause to reconsider how that tactic will be implemented.

Once you have settled on a set of tactics and combined them into one program, ask yourself the following questions:

- How does the complete program help us address each of the challenges specified?
- Can we generate data from the program in a way that gives us a holistic view of performance?
- Do we have a project/program manager who understands each of the tactics well enough to oversee the execution of this program?

Upon completion, this section will equip you with a blueprint for creating a cohesive, well-thought-out program for dealing with marketing challenges. Rather than being designed solely to help you choose marketing channels or tactics, this section, when optimally used, helps you create a program that ensures you are demonstrating success to those who hold you accountable. Additionally, by verifying that your program addresses your challenges and provides a holistic view of your performance, you essentially ensure your tactics integrate well—improving your likelihood of success.

Result	**Goal:** Identify the quantitative and qualitative metrics that will be used to gauge the success of the project and the stages at which those metrics will be measured. **Approach:** After the Situation section, this is the most important component of this document. Many projects fail to achieve their goals because the objectives were never clearly delineated at the outset. When done well, the content of this section establishes precisely what benefits the organization should have achieved over the course of the program. One way to begin this section is by returning to the Situation section and reviewing your challenges. Then, approach each challenge qualitatively and quantitatively. For example, qualitatively, you might conclude that you need to increase revenue generated by your website and establish increased conversions as a way of doing that. Quantitatively, however, you would improve your precision and say, *We need a 23 percent lift in conversions at our current average transaction prices to achieve our goal of increasing revenue by 40 percent.* The benefits of precision are many. They ensure that all project stakeholders share the same ideas about project goals. Additionally, they help those developing the solution match their efforts to the project's objectives. Finally, they are a tool for measuring performance, potentially enabling you to adjust the project's in-market assets in real time to account for negative or positive differences between expected and actual performance.

	Successfully filling out this section can be determined by assessing whether there are both quantitative and qualitative metrics of measuring the challenges you stated in the Situation section. Be mindful that you are not limited to one metric per challenge. You can have as many metrics per challenge as is warranted. Be mindful, however, that each metric gauged adds complexity. The ultimate solution should be capable of tracking each metric, and your team should have the ability to manage and effectively use the data being generated.

Upon completing the STAIR, you should have a clear and well-thought-out explanation of your requirements. Someone coming in off the street should be able to read this single document and understand what you intend to do, why you want to do it, and the outcome you desire. The cynic might be inclined to opine, "Well, no one is coming in off the street." This is probably true, but as a modern marketer, you will undoubtedly rely on multiple people on your own team, colleagues from other departments, and vendors to execute your project.

The STAIR establishes a line in the sand from which everyone moves forward with the same information and provides a target toward which they can aim. It is the project's mission statement, and by going through the process of building it, you help coalesce your entire team around a common vision and, hopefully, increase the likelihood of success.

CHAPTER 12

TECHNOLOGY SUCCESS AND FAILURE

If having a clearly defined mission were the only ingredient necessary to achieve success with technology-dependent projects, there would be a lot fewer bottles of painkillers and antacids in the drawers of information technology personnel. Pitfalls (and headaches) abound.

Problems arise during execution that delay or derail even the most mission-critical projects. In fact, within technology circles, it is thought that most (60–85 percent, in fact) technology projects that fail to meet their objectives are delayed or exceed their budget.[lix] As a marketer, to limit the impact of the obstacles and risks that can sideline your projects, you must be aware of the pitfalls associated with running technology-dependent projects.

Most of the key points of failure for technology projects are already familiar to marketers. They do not differ substantially for technology-based projects. Still, they are worth reviewing here as a reminder of the dangers that can sink your important projects. The most common causes of technology project failure include the following:[lx]

- **Lack of commitment from senior management**–Just as the project manager is responsible for stewarding the project through the obstacle course often associated with executing technology-based projects, someone in the organization must see the project through the political environment of the organization. The absence of this person—or a general feeling from management that the project has little value—can be a project killer.

- **Poor planning**–I have come across very few projects in my career that didn't have a high priority to someone and that weren't needed by some seemingly impossible date. It's the nature of marketing projects. The result of this "need it yesterday" environment is that project managers are often asked to get a project underway before they've had enough time to adequately assess the project's needs, gauge its risks, and plan accordingly. Neglecting to adequately plan, however, is a large component of the recipe for failure.

- **Unclear or changing goals and objectives**–As mentioned earlier, one important benefit of the STAIR is that it establishes a way to ensure all project participants begin the project with the same understanding of the project's goals. By doing so, people working on the project can develop solutions that align with the project's objectives. Unclear objectives or those that change over the course of the project require the team to reevaluate their earlier thinking, potentially leading to dissension and definitely resulting in an expanding schedule. Stick to your guns and update goals and objectives in the next phase.

- **Inaccurate time and resource estimates**–Every project, regardless of discipline, lives and dies by its time and resource estimates. It is challenging to recover from improperly gauging either metric. Yet, project managers are often under pressure to achieve project goals and, as a result, improperly estimate what's necessary to complete the project. Project managers should be trained to use proven methodologies for gauging time and resources. Additionally, as a manger, you should trust the time and resource estimates received from your project managers. Applying unnecessary pressure can have unintended (and unwanted) consequences.

- **Lack of communication**–In the drive to achieve their individual goals, teams on many projects have the potential to not communicate with each other. Communication is often not scheduled as a formal activity on anyone's calendar, and so it does not happen. This lack of communication can result in no one having a complete view of the project's progress or its challenges. This ultimately leads to unwanted surprises that can doom your project. Ensuring your project manager schedules routine meetings between project leads and using a shared project management tool can encourage communication between teams.

- **Inadequate experience and training**–Your team should have the know-how and experience to pull off the type of project you have tasked them with. Ask yourself, Has my project manager managed this type of project before? Can I identify individuals on my team who have specific skills with the technology we are using? For technology-dependent projects, your staff will often need both breadth and depth of skill to successfully execute the project. Where the skills don't exist, rather than trust your team can learn on the job, either send them for training or hire staff familiar with the technology who can transfer knowledge to your team.

So, there are plenty of potential hazards that await the marketer engaging in the creation of technology-based solutions. Technology is both the present and future of marketing, however, so you must meet these hazards head on. This requires working with your team and your management to mitigate the risks described above. Additionally, getting a handle on these projects requires having a firm understanding about the process of getting technology-based projects from ideation to implementation.

Software Development/Product Development Process

Whether we acknowledge it or not, process plays a big part in everything we do in life. Generally, however, we take it for granted—underestimating its importance to our daily activities. It is unfortunate, really, that process is so overlooked. It is key to events going as we expect. If we shift our car's transmission into drive before starting it, or even put on our raincoat *after* going out in the rain, we change the order of two proven processes in a way that makes the end result less effective. Process is a means to a successful end for cars and raincoats just as it is for marketing and technology.

As a professional marketer, you likely have a process to which you adhere when developing a new program. Your process may differ slightly from your colleague in another department or at another company. The specifics of the process, however, follow a sequential path that involves performing a series of steps that build upon the previous steps so you can move to the next phase of execution. Technologists rely on the same type of processes to develop software projects.

> **! SPECIAL NOTE**
>
> AS A MARKETER, YOU MAY BE THINKING THAT A LOT OF WHAT I HAVE SHARED IN THIS CHAPTER IS VERY TECHNICAL. IT MAY BE. THAT IS EXACTLY THE POINT I WANT TO GET ACROSS. MARKETING IS CHANGING AT LIGHT SPEED. A SIGNIFICANT AMOUNT OF THAT CHANGE IS A RESULT OF TECHNOLOGY'S INFLUENCE ON THE DISCIPLINE. TODAY'S MARKETER (NOT TOMORROW'S BECAUSE TOMORROW IS HERE ALREADY) MUST BE KNOWLEDGEABLE ABOUT NOT JUST THE TACTICS BUT ALSO THE PROCESSES FOR ACHIEVING HIS GOALS.
>
> I KNOW SOMEONE WHO ASKED HER PLUMBER FOR ADVICE ON HAVING HER BOILER REPLACED IN HER HOME. THE PLUMBER SUGGESTED THAT SHE GO OUT TO A BOOKSTORE AND PURCHASE A BOOK ON FURNACES AND THEN READ THE BOOK. THEY BOTH KNEW SHE WOULD NOT END UP AN EXPERT ON FURNACES. SHE WOULD, HOWEVER, BE WELL VERSED ENOUGH TO HAVE A WELL-INFORMED CONVERSATION WITH A HEATING SPECIALIST AND AVOID BEING FLEECED. MUCH OF THIS CHAPTER, AND IN FACT THE BOOK, IS ABOUT ARMING YOURSELF WITH INFORMATION YOU CAN WIELD AS YOU GO FORTH AND BUILD BETTER, MORE POWERFUL TECHNOLOGY-ENABLED MARKETING PROGRAMS.

In fact, information technology professionals and consultants generally rely on one of two approaches when developing technology-centric projects:

- Waterfall Model–The tried and true, traditional approach to development is very similar to the standard marketing process in that it is sequential. Each successive phase relies on information and assets created in the prior phase. See Figure 7.

- Agile Development–Newer approach that reduces the dependence on traditional detailed requirements and instead relies on frequent iterations of the software to elicit client feedback. Doing so can result in an improved final product and quicker time to market. See Figure 8.

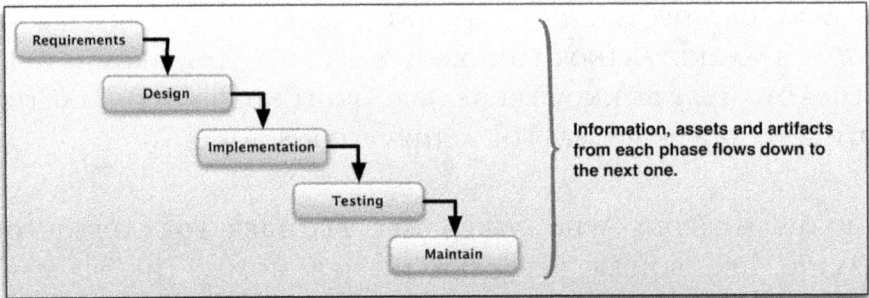

FIGURE 7. WATERFALL MODEL

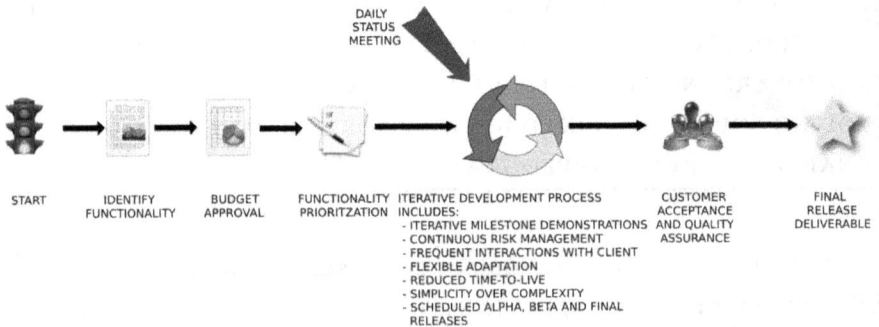

FIGURE 8. AGILE DEVELOPMENT PROCESS

The two processes are very different. The waterfall model relies on a significant number of assets and documents that are generated over the course of the project to ensure that the final product reflects the sponsor's vision. The agile development process, on the other hand, relies on frequent sponsor engagement and, as the name of the process implies, agility to produce your finished product.

As a marketer and the likely sponsor of technology-dependent projects, you may be thinking to yourself that the agile process has clear benefits over the waterfall model. Who could blame you? In reality, however, while the two processes are frequently interchangeable, it is often best to consider your objectives before having your project team arbitrarily commit to using either approach.

The linear methodology of the waterfall model makes it a strong candidate for projects where deadlines are rigid or where the project team finds difficulty with flexibility. Additionally, using the waterfall model can provide the perception of reduced risk due to the thorough planning necessary to adequately manage the staged phases of the process. This approach may also be beneficial when you have very well-defined requirements or when you are faced with a one-time implementation (such as with a CRM system). Finally, this approach may be best when working with teams who have lengthy experience with it and for whom retraining is impractical. It is, after all, the long established traditional approach for technology projects.

Where the waterfall model necessitates rigidity and very thorough planning, the agile process puts greater priority on efficiency and client-team interactions. Rather than identifying requirements and then building a product that is revealed to the project sponsor at the end of the process (as is the case with the waterfall model), the agile methodology takes advantage of frequent interactions and rapid product iterations to quickly deliver solutions. The agile approach is especially appropriate for web-based applications as they will be likely to go through a series of frequent updates in which functionality is added. Agile is also appropriate when the timeline for building a new solution is compressed, as the process allows the production/development team to begin showing progress shortly after beginning execution. This relatively new approach will undoubtedly be unfamiliar to many teams, but it may revolutionize the way your project team accomplishes its goals.

I realize that, as the marketer, you will have little influence over what type of approach the technology team of your ad agency or your company's IT team uses when building a new solution. Both groups will use the most familiar approach. My goal in this section, however, has been to ensure that you are well armed with the information you need to understand what happens with either approach—and to recognize the approaches by whatever name the technology team refers to their proprietary methodology. By being aware, you are empowered to better gauge your projects' progress regardless of how the team building it approaches the build.

lix. http://www.bizjournals.com/portland/stories/2008/10/20/smallb4.html?page=all.

lx. http://149.144.20.200/subjects/ISD/isds111web/WhyDoITProjectsFail.pdf

CHAPTER 13

CONCLUSION

Have you ever watched the television show, *Revolution*? It's a post-apocalyptic series that takes place after a blackout strips the world of electricity. The world of *Revolution* is one in which people have to adapt to not having electrical power. It's like living in the nineteenth century. I am not endorsing the show (though it can be entertaining). In some ways, I imagine going back to the days before digital technologies so radically changed marketing would be a bit like losing electricity. As long as the power stays on, technology is now inextricably intertwined with marketing. From my perspective, that is a very good thing.

After all, the benefits of the marriage between marketing and technology are numerous. Campaigns are more measurable than ever. You can directly engage individual customers and inquire about how they feel about your brand. It is possible to track behavior across your site and even link site activity to real-world actions. Forward-thinking marketers are using multiple data sources—so called "big data"—to glean insight from customers' behaviors, and they use those insights to create more profitable campaigns. Not to mention, you can personalize your message and deliver custom content to users so that it precisely matches the touchpoint they use to engage your brand. All of this is huge. Not big. *Huge.*

In writing this book, I opted to cover a few of the topics that I believe matter most to marketers looking to *Get Digital*—among them how to think strategically about digital, understanding the options that exist for specific needs, and how to approach integrating marketing and technology in a way that works for your team. There are plenty of topics that space and time did not allow me to cover. Some of them—big data, for example—are likely to be presented in a *Get Digital* series e-book. Others, like e-mail and search, are long enough in the tooth that I presume most marketers interested in them can avail themselves of the many resources available both online and in book form. I would encourage the marketer interested in any of these topics to pursue the other resources that are available.

I find the following sources to be helpful in keeping track of what's happening in the industry:

Site Name	URL
AdAge	adage.com
All Things D	allthingsd.com
ArsTechnica	arstechnica.com
Forrester CMO Blog	blogs.forrester.com/cmo
Forrester Marketing Leadership Blog	blogs.forrester.com/interactive_marketing
GigaOm	gigaom.com
Marketing Land	marketingland.com
PaidContent	paidcontent.org
TechCrunch	techcrunch.com
TechMeme	techmeme.com

VentureBeat	venturebeat.com
Bloomberg News	www.bloomberg.com/news
Business Insider	www.businessinsider.com
Chief Marketer	www.chiefmarketer.com
CMSWire	www.cmswire.com
Forbes Technology Blog	www.forbes.com/technology
Marketing Charts	www.marketingcharts.com
MarketingProfs	www.marketingprofs.com
Marketing Sherpa	www.marketingsherpa.com
MediaPost Publications News	www.mediapost.com/publications
TechDirt	www.techdirt.com
The Verge	www.theverge.com

Thank you for taking the time to read this book. Please stay tuned for more books in the *Get Digital* series as this is just the first of what I hope will be a series that marketers come to trust for guidance on digital technologies.

In the meantime, you can always find me on Twitter with username @talibmorgan or @marketnology. You can also contact me on the Contact Us page on my company's website: www.actuanglobal.com.

www.ingramcontent.com/pod-product-compliance
Lightning Source LLC
Chambersburg PA
CBHW070929210326
41520CB00021B/6854